DATE DUE

NOV 1			
NOV 22 1999			
GAYLORD			PRINTED IN U.S.A.

TWICE QUEEN OF FRANCE

Anne of Brittany

ANNE OF BRITTANY

TWICE QUEEN
OF FRANCE

Anne of Brittany

Mildred Allen Butler

Portraits by Bette Davis

FUNK & WAGNALLS
A Division of Reader's Digest Books, Inc.
NEW YORK

AUTHOR'S NOTE

The date of Anne's birth is given as 1477 in three encyclopedias: the Brittanica, the Columbia, and the French Larousse. However, the three French accounts dealing with her entire life in detail and based on nearly contemporary memoirs, one by Brantôme and one by Commynges, give 1476 as her birth date. This date is further authenticated by statements of her age at the date of her marriages, to Charles and to Louis, and at the date of her death.

The name of Anne's sister Isabeau, which is the masculine form of Isabelle, was not unusual during the Renaissance. Isabeau is given as the name of a daughter of a royal house in several countries, among them, the house of Castile.

Until the Renaissance, white was worn for mourning by the nobility and royalty, and black by the lower classes. Anne changed this, as far as France was concerned, by wearing black in mourning for Charles VIII. Earlier, when her sister died, she wore white.

Among the volumes consulted in my preparation for this biography of Anne of Brittany, in addition to the encyclopedias just mentioned are:

Leroux de Lincy, A. J. V.: *Vie de la reine Anne de Bretagne* (4 vol. 1860–61)

Bailly, Auguste: *Anne de Bretagne, Reine de France* (Paris, Les Éditions de France, 1940)

Toudouze, Georges: *Anne, Duchesse de Bretagne, Reine de France* (André Bonne, France, 1959)

De la Warr, Constance: *A Twice Crowned Queen, Anne of Brittany* (New York, D. Appleton, 1907)

Bearne, C. M.: *Pictures of the Old French Court* (New York, Dutton, 1900)

Bourdichons, Jehan: *Les Heures d'Anne de Bretagne* (Pictures selected from the *Book of Hours*.) (Editions Verve, Paris, 1946)

Brock, Emma Lillian: *The Little Duchess, Anne of Brittany* (New York, Knopf, 1948)

Duby, Georges, and Mandron, Robert: *History of French Civilization* (New York, Random House, 1964)

Funck-Brentano: *The Renaissance* (New York, Macmillan, 1936)

Charles, Pierre: *L'Histoire d'Amboise* (Tours, France, no date)

Checksfield, N. M.: *Portraits of Renaissance Life and Thought* (New York, Longmans, 1964)

Contents

TWICE QUEEN OF FRANCE

Anne of Brittany

CHAPTER I

Childhood of a Duchess

ANNE STOOD IN A WINDOW EMBRASURE of the small Château de Coiron. She was gazing vacantly at the blue and gray slate roofs of the stone cottages that, facing in all directions, crowded against the chateau, where the Duke of Brittany and his court were staying because the plague raged at Nantes.

Slight of figure and scarcely five feet tall, Anne wore a tight-fitting green bodice with short draped skirt over a flowing gown of blue. Her long dark hair was covered with a Breton cape—a softly hanging scarf, also green, lined at the face with a band of white linen. Beside her stood the haughty, yet beloved Madame de Dinan, her governess, cousin, and friend, who was wearing a more elaborate dress of yellow and purple.

In another room, Anne's father lay dying. He had escaped the plague only to be taken with a fatal fever. How sad, she thought, that he could not be in their own beautiful home, the Château de Nantes, which he loved so dearly. As she wiped away the tears that occasionally slipped down her cheeks, Madame whispered, "Have courage, my child. It is not yet the end."

Footsteps in the stone corridor and the sound of the far door opening made them both turn. Two lackeys entered and stood aside to admit Philippe de Montauban, Baron de Grenouville and Chancellor of Brittany. He walked slowly to the window, fell on one knee before Anne, and pressed his lips to her hand.

"Your Grace," he said, "it is over." Then, rising, he announced in a formal and reverent tone: "Francis II, Duke of Brittany is dead. God rest his soul." He crossed himself and stepped back, his head bowed.

Anne's eyes overflowed with tears, but she managed to control her grief. "You called me 'Your Grace'!"

"Yes, my lady. Your Highness is now Duchess of Brittany and our Sovereign Lady. May God preserve you!"

Turning to her governess, Anne cried, "Alas, Madame! Our hope is gone. It is indeed the end." She leaned against Madame de Dinan for a moment of comfort, then straightened. "I must go to my father's bedside and take my leave of him. But first, my sister Isabeau must be told. She is in the garden."

"I will send a page," Madame de Dinan said.

"No," replied Anne, "I will go myself. She will cry, and I must comfort her."

As she crossed the room, Philippe de Montauban placed himself before her and knelt once more at her feet. "Your Grace," he said with unmistakable sincerity, "if you are in need of a friend, now that you are ruler, remember that you can count on me. Only death can prevent my serving you as I served your father, and even more faithfully, for you will need me more."

"You have my thanks, Baron," answered Anne gravely. "Indeed I know that I can depend on you, at least." She threw back her shoulders and walked with a firm step, her limp scarcely noticeable, to the massive carved door. The two lackeys bowed low before her.

Anne, Duchess of Brittany, was just twelve years old.

When she had found her sister, sitting pensively on the coping of the lily pool with her nurse watchfully standing by, Anne gently told her what had happened and said that they must go to take a last farewell of the father they had loved so dearly. Frail little Isabeau clung to her, weeping, and the nurse threw her apron over her face and rocked back and forth, sobbing loudly.

Anne took Isabeau by the hand, and together they entered the chateau and climbed the stone stairway to their father's apartments. Light from the high windows fell in squares on the corridor, but though the autumn sunshine was warm, it made little impression on the chill of the interior. Lackeys admitted them to the Duke's chamber, where thick draperies had been drawn over the windows. Lighted candelabra stood on carved walnut chests about the room and on stands around the bed, filling the room with a flickering, golden light. In one corner, the Bishop of Condon and three priests talked in low tones, preparing for the private mass that would be celebrated later in the chapel.

Francis II of Brittany lay peacefully, his eyes closed. The anxieties of the last years of his reign, which his daughter Anne knew very well, had all slipped away. A cloth of gold coverlet had been drawn up to his chin, and with features softened and relaxed, he looked as though he were asleep. His daughter knelt by the bedside.

"My dear father," said Anne, tears choking her, for she knew that he could not hear her now, "I shall do my best to rule the land as you have done—to keep peace within Brittany and to repel the French who would conquer us."

The Bishop crossed to her. "Take comfort," he said. "He did not suffer, and he died in the state of grace."

After a lingering look at the still figure in the ducal bed, the children bowed to the Bishop and went out, their tiny handkerchiefs of Holland linen pressed to their eyes. But as they passed the group of weeping servants who had gathered in the hall, Anne held her head high, for she was now their duchess and would soon wear the crown that had been handed down since the year 845, when the Duchy of Brittany had first become a sovereign state. They must not see her cry!

Anne's domain was the whole peninsula of Brittany, which had been called Amorica when it was invaded by the Romans many centuries before. It thrust west from the mainland into the Atlantic Ocean, forming the northern arm of the Bay of Biscay, as Spain formed the southern arm. To the north lay the islands of Jersey, Guernsey, and Alderney, and at its most northern point it was not far across the channel to Cornwall on the island of Britain. From Cornwall, in the fourth and fifth centuries, had come a peaceful invasion of great numbers of Celtic people fleeing from the Saxon barbarians who had invaded their territory. So many had come, in fact, that the peninsula became known as Little Britain—Brittany. It was a country of contrasts, barren and rocky in parts, very fertile in others, and its people were proud and fiercely independent. Considered a rich prize for any king or baron who could conquer it, it was in a most hazardous position and was a grave responsibility for a little duchess.

On the twenty-sixth of January, 1476, twelve years before the death of Duke Francis, bells pealed joyfully from all the towers in the city of Nantes, for, at last, to the beloved Duke a child was born. All had hoped for a son, but in Brittany a girl-child might inherit the crown, so the people rejoiced because the succession was now assured. The townspeople, in holiday attire, paraded from the central square to the chateau and back again through the narrow streets to the cathedral to offer thanks for their good fortune. They had almost given up hope because Francis II, twice married and forty years of age, had until then been childless. Now, when the time should come for death to take him from them, they would not be gobbled up by a neighboring duchy. Now there was a daughter of his blood who would rule them—as kindly, they were sure, as he had ruled. The birth of his heir was indeed an occasion for singing and dancing in the streets.

It was a no less happy event for Francis' wife, Marguerite de Foix. As was the custom, Francis had a favorite among the ladies of the court, and Marguerite had felt neglected. As the mother of the heir to the throne, she no longer had any need to feel inferior to the Duke's favorite, and she turned her full attention to bringing up this daughter as befitted a princess.

In the early Renaissance, all Europe was composed of small units, some of them closely allied, but each burning with national fervor and the will to survive. The ruler of each lived in as much magnificence as he could find money for, and because all these units had once been kingdoms, dukes were often called princes or even kings. So it was that Francis' little daughter would live as a princess.

The baby was named Anne, after the most holy saint of Brittany, and her christening in the cathedral at Nantes was a solemn event marked by a great procession: priests in colorful robes, carrying the gilded image of Saint Anne, an elaborate crucifix, and other symbols of the church; next the nobles of Brittany, in rich attire, attended by squires holding aloft pennants decorated with their personal crests; and finally the townspeople and peasants in their best clothes.

"Long life to the Duchess Anne!" cried the people. But among themselves they whispered, "If she will only live to grow up!" Dangerous as were the enemies from without the duchy, the most feared of all was the sudden illness that so often struck a child quite soon after its birth. In the fifteenth century, doctors knew so little that few children in a family lived to grow up. A son, born to Francis by his first wife, had lived only a few days. It would be a terrible blow to the people of Brittany if their little duchess did not survive.

In full knowledge of this danger, Francis sent for a woman of Rennes, the second largest town of his duchy, who had been recommended to him as a nurse for Anne. But a few days after the arrival of Demoiselle de la Vire, the doctors, noting the way she handled the infant, shook their heads and declared that she would not do—Anne must have more expert care. After further inquiries, another nurse was found—a woman named Jean Eon. Of her the doctors approved, and she took such excellent care of her charge, keeping her warm and well fed, clean and out of drafts, that Jean Eon stayed on in the Duke's service for many years.

Anne was a sweet-faced baby with a winning smile, and she was almost perfect in form—this in a day when it was so common for children to be born with deformities or even dwarf-like stature, that a mother thanked God with particular fervor if she bore a perfectly developed child. Anne did have one defect that became evident only when she learned to walk. One leg was a trifle shorter than the other, which gave her a slight limp. This did not bother her at all; she grew up with it and learned to compensate. It was, of course, never mentioned in her presence by her nurse or the courtiers, and when she grew older she taught herself to walk almost evenly by rising slightly on the toes of one foot.

She was a happy child, though strong-willed and not amenable to discipline. As the first child in a royal household, her every wish was granted. Perhaps she might have been a spoiled child, and she certainly would have been a very lonely one, if it had not been that, happily, another girl was born to Francis and Marguerite when Anne was two years old. From the beginning, the second daughter was a sickly child and all the care lavished on her did not greatly help. She was named Isabeau. When she grew older, Anne had a companion, and the sisters were devoted to each other. Their mother gave nearly all of her time to her daughters, and they loved her dearly. In like manner they loved their father, for although Francis spent much of his leisure with his court favorites, he became increasingly interested in the welfare of his children and did everything he could to please them. The opulence of his court, the beauty of the chateau he had built at Nantes, and the art treasures he collected made a rich background of Renaissance culture in which Anne, particularly, flourished.

A governess for the children was selected with great care. Francis wanted them to have a literary education—rare for women at that time—so that they might appreciate the library he had accumulated. He was among the first of the dukes of central Europe to take an interest in things of beauty —paintings, sculpture, and classic manuscripts. He founded schools, encouraged commerce, and brought artists and tapestry workers from Flanders to embellish his chateau. Although for most of his lifetime he struggled against aggression by force of arms, Francis was not a warlike man.

It was a cousin who was finally chosen to be governess. She was Françoise de Dinan of the family of Albret, with the title of Dame de Chateaubriand and Laval, and she was a great lady with courteous manners, a knowledge of court etiquette indispensable to the future duchess, and an erudition unusual for a woman. She came to live at the palace and took over the education of the girls. Anne was very quick and intelligent; but Isabeau, because of frail health, could not participate in much that was offered and had to spend many hours in bed, too weak even to talk.

To look at the chateau of Nantes from the river, one would scarcely think there could be a green area where children might play. It was built high above the river Loire, from which rose a long solid wall forty feet high, topped by another wall with round towers at each end. These were the fortifications. Fronting the chateau, the grand loge—the main building—rose eight stories from the ground. It had two small set-in balconies in the upper stories from which Anne used to look out over the city. If it was market day, or a juggler was attracting a crowd, or a procession of mendicant friars was passing through on a pilgrimage, it was a fine spot to watch from without being seen. Two wings from the grand palace stretched back to join the river walls, thus providing a secluded courtyard and garden of beautiful trees, which covered several acres. There, guarded by a special group of soldiers and watched over by both governess and nurse, it was safe, even in those perilous days, for the children to play.

Because Madame de Dinan was highly educated, she was able to teach Anne a great deal, including a reading knowledge of Latin and Greek, which the governess considered important as a background of culture and worthwhile as a mental discipline. Thanks to her, Anne, who was unusually responsive, could write as well as read and, what is more important, think things through wisely. She was taught to appreciate music and painting, to sing, dance, embroider, and make lace. Anne also learned how to keep accounts and manage a household, abilities as necessary to a sovereign as to a housewife.

But sometimes Anne was allowed to be just a child. Despite her limp, she flew about on nimble feet as she romped and played. Isabeau was passive and grave, and Anne often slowed to the pace of her more delicate sister. Both girls were fond of animals, and there were always pet dogs about and cages full of songbirds.

The sisters had a playmate in their half-brother Antoine, only a little older than Anne, who was so full of pranks that the courtiers called him "Antoine the Mischief-Maker." Besides Antoine, but older, there were two others, François d'Avougour and Françoise. All three were the children of Francis II by his court favorite, Antoinette de Maignelais. Though they were socially accepted by everyone, as was the custom, no one of them could have inherited the duchy. It was for this reason that Francis was considered childless until the birth of Anne, his legal heir.

For the most part, lessons were conducted in one of the halls of the castle. "You must learn to walk like a duchess," Madame de Dinan would tell Anne. "See!" The lady would walk majestically, her head up, trailing her silken skirts, and four-year-old Anne, also in long skirts, would follow, stepping with grown-up dignity. Much that she was taught to master was far beyond her years, but in an era when life was short, royal children had to take on responsibilities at an early age. Who knew when Anne would have to stop playing and become a ruling duchess? "Extend your hand to be kissed," commanded her governess, illustrating the pose, and little Anne, drawing herself up to her height of three feet, would hold out her hand to an imaginary courtier.

She began the study of Latin and Greek when she was only four years old. There were few writings in any other language, although some of the manuscripts in the Duke's library were in French—a language she soon mastered and could read and write as easily as her native tongue. Not only was French the language of France, Brittany's powerful neighbor; since the Norman Conquest in 1066, it had been used exclusively at the court of England. The Breton dialect was spoken and sung by troubadours who came to Brittany, and some romances were written in that dialect, which was of Celtic origin. But serious manuscripts and books were in the classical languages or in French. Anne must learn to read the contents of her father's library—it was expected of her, and it was her own desire. This she did not find very difficult, and she soon astonished her father with her proficiency. Indeed, as the news of the accomplished princess spread throughout the duchy, several learned books were dedicated "to the Princess Anne."

At that time, most of the manuscripts in a nobleman's library had been painstakingly written by hand on vellum or parchment made from the finest skins of lamb, goat, or calf. The work was done by monks or by lay brothers—men who had kept alive in the monasteries the culture of Greece and Rome during Europe's dark ages. Often, starting the first word of a chapter was a large letter painted in green, red, or blue, embellished with gold, the skillful and artistic work of a dedicated brother. Each manuscript took years to complete.

In 1476, printing was still in its infancy, having been invented only twenty-five years before, in Germany. And in 1476, the year of Anne's birth, William Caxton set up the first printing press in England. But printing, too, was a laborious business. Each page was set by hand and printed separately, with infinite labor, on a hand press. Hence, a printed book was still very rare indeed. When Anne was a child, manuscripts were far more common, for churchmen had been at work copying them ever since the Fall of Rome ten centuries before. Many could be bought by the wealthy aristocracy, and others were seized by military leaders when they conquered a city.

When not studying with her governess, Anne and her little sister were watched over by their nurse. Nurse Eon had a head full of legends and folk tales with which she amused her charges. She also had a real belief in fairies and goblins, who, she said, inhabited the forests and swamps, meeting mortals and leading them into peril. Anne shivered with delighted horror at the tales of "fairy rings" into which no one dared step, of children who were changelings, of quests for enchanted objects that could lead the adventurer into great danger, and of witches and their evil spells. The Breton folklore did not tell of good fairies like the "little people" of Irish legend. Perhaps because of the large rocks and wild moorlands that made up a great part of Brittany and created a gloomy atmosphere, the peasants believed that all fairies were wicked, casting spells on human beings, stealing from them, and becoming invisible or changing their shapes at will. Even the beautiful forest of Brocéliande, in which King Arthur's knights were supposed to have roamed seeking adventure, was believed to be full of evil fairies, and brave was the peasant who ventured there.

Although Anne was exceptionally intelligent, it was natural for her in her childhood to accept the legends that the greater part of her people believed wholeheartedly. When she and Isabeau asked for a story, their nurse could tell them any of dozens of tales—and all of them, she would assure the girls, were absolutely true because she had heard them from her grandmother, who had heard them from *her* grandmother, and so on back to the beginning of time! If so many people had known these stories, how could they *not* be true?

An endless number told how a young man of lowly birth, after undergoing incredible hardships and accomplishing miraculous adventures, was finally rewarded by marrying a princess. That was the favorite theme. There was the tale of the Princess Starbright, who promised a miller three sacks of gold and three sacks of silver if he would free her from enchantment by spending three nights in a ruined manor house supposed to be haunted by devils. He did as she asked; each night he was tortured by a dozen devils, and each morning his wounds were healed by the princess. On the fourth morning, she gave him the treasure she had promised; and finally, after more adventures with magic apples, enchanted gaiters, and a hidden casket, she rewarded the miller for his courage on her behalf by becoming his wife.

Another story concerned the twenty-sixth son of a charcoal burner who was under obligation to the king who had acted as godfather when the boy was baptized. When grown to young manhood, he was tricked into searching for the reason why the sun looked so red when it rose. He mounted a magic steed and flew on him up to the sun, which had the appearance of a man in kingly garments. When the youth questioned him, the sun replied that there was a beautiful princess, named the Princess Tronkolaine, who looked for him each morning in the eastern sky and he wished to look his best. When the king heard this, he demanded that his godson find the princess and bring her to him to be his queen. In attempting to do so, the youth started on a quest that involved three ships—one of oatmeal, one of bacon, and one of salt meat—and three islands—one of ants, one of lions, and one of sparrow hawks. He befriended the creatures, and they in turn befriended him so that he found the Princess Tronkolaine and took her to the king. But instead of marrying the king, she preferred to marry the young man, and they lived happily ever after.

The imagination of countless generations of peasants had gone into these tales, which reflected the very understandable desire of the lowly to escape the class into which they had been born and find the happiness that they imagined was enjoyed by the kings and princes who ruled them.

In addition, there were other types of stories about knights and ladies where the emphasis was upon courage in battle and brave deeds that delivered damsels in distress from wicked knights. Of these, the most widely known were the tales of King Arthur Pendragon and his Knights of the Round Table, of Merlin the Magician, and of Parsifal and the search for the Holy Grail. In Britain, the legendary home of King Arthur was Camelot in Cornwall, but the Bretons thought that the Knights of the Round Table roamed their forest of Brocéliande.

Anne and Isabeau listened to the nurse's tales with great enjoyment. Not all of them ended with "living happily ever after." They were exciting stories and sometimes frightening, and Nurse Eon said they were *true*. There was, for instance, the eerie tale of the city of Ys on the northern coast of Brittany, which sank suddenly into the ocean many, many years ago, and can still be seen by true believers—its towers deep in the green sea off the rocky shore. When the wind is right, the sound of church bells floats inland, whereupon the credulous ones cross themselves, remembering the fate of that beautiful city lost now beneath the waves.

Most often, storytime came when dusk fell early and the tapestries were lifted from the walls with each gust of wind that found its way through the casements. Anne and her sister would sit with Nurse Eon on the floor before the huge, carved stone fireplace in their apartment of the chateau. At the end of the evening, the two sleepy little girls would leave the firelit room for their bedchamber on the floor above. They were escorted by pages in red doublets and yellow hose, who carried torches that cast flickering shadows on the walls— frightening shadows. However, Nurse Eon came right along with her arms about the girls' shoulders and her skirts billowing close so that they might feel protected from goblins and evil spirits—or, more realistically, from the mice and rats that often scurried along the stone corridors. In the bedroom that they shared, the children slept in a high, canopied bed with blue and gold velvet curtains that were kept tightly closed so that no breath of air could cause a chill, even though, according to ancient custom, the casements were firmly shut to keep out the fresh night breezes. Nurse's bed was in one corner of the large chamber, and the girls were not afraid, knowing nothing, in their early innocence, of dangers greater than witchcraft—danger from traitors with daggers or poison, or from serious illness that could threaten life.

Anne's first years passed happily. There were the church festivals, which she loved both for their pageantry and because they satisfied an innate spiritual need. There were gay parties in the castle or, when it was safe, in the woodlands surrounding it, which were attended by neighboring lords and their families. Sometimes wandering troubadours came to sing their songs of love and adventure, of war and death. Every day she pursued studies that awakened her eager mind, and there was always Nurse Eon to tell a story by the fire in the evening.

CHAPTER II

Brittany in Danger

AT THE TIME of the birth of Anne of Brittany, the lands that now comprise France, the Netherlands, Germany, Austria, and Italy had not yet coalesced into the monarchies they eventually became. They consisted of duchies, the more powerful of which were called kingdoms and, in Italy, city states. They were all at war with one another from time to time, for each was eager to acquire more territory and more control. England, though separated from the mainland, was the ally of first one duke and then another, and for a hundred years laid claim to nearly all of the French duchies. France, whose King Louis XI was continually fighting on the north with Burgundy, on the east with Austria, and on the west with Brittany, did not succeed in driving out the English armies until close to the end of the fifteenth century. Anne was born only a few years after Joan of Arc had turned the tide in favor of the French. Believing through her visions that a king ruled by divine right, Joan had persuaded the worthless Charles VII, predecessor of Louis, to go to Rheims to be crowned, thus hastening the decline of the power of the dukes and barons.

The institution known as feudalism was coming to an end, and the age of the monarchy was at hand, along with the rise of the middle class of tradesmen. As new routes to old lands were opened, merchants became wealthy, and it was from them that the princes borrowed heavily to finance their wars. Although Europe was still a land divided into the holdings of many barons, who built strongly fortified castles to defend their territory and had the power of life and death over all their inhabitants, there was a new spirit in the air—a new interest in art, in letters, and in exploration. It was called the Renaissance.

Duke Francis of Brittany may not have been aware of the long-range changes taking place in Europe, but he was all too constantly reminded that King Louis of France was trying to add Brittany to the provinces already within his grasp. While Anne was growing up, her country was deeply involved in intrigues, invaded by spies, plotted against, betrayed by traitors, and, not infrequently, forced to fight pitched battles on its own soil. Though she could scarcely have understood what she might have overheard of all this, she became aware of her father's devotion to Breton independence and the role she was expected to play when, at the age of five, she was betrothed to Prince Edward of England, son of Edward IV. She was the central figure in a solemn ceremony that cemented the alliance of Brittany and England against their common enemy, the King of France. According to the agreement, the marriage ceremony was to take place when Anne was twelve years old.

That was a long way off, however, and many alliances were to be made and broken in the next seven years.

Among the provinces that owed allegiance to France, although they were not a part of the French kingdom, Brittany was unique. From the time of Clovis, it had had a king as ruler; and though, with the advent of the powerful Hugh Capet, it had been forced to recognize the sovereignty of France, the only change was in its title—the kingdom became a duchy. The duke held his power, not from France, but from God. The Breton rulers were not obliged to go through the ceremony of rendering absolute homage to the king of France. Therefore, when Francis II, crowned at Rennes in 1459, went to pay his respects to Charles VII of France, he was not required to kneel. The King's counsellor demanded, however, that Francis take off his sword.

To this the Duke's chancellor replied, "That would be a departure from custom. It has not been done this way."

"But, Monseigneur de Bretagne," the French official said to Francis, "you must pledge allegiance to the King, your sovereign lord, on behalf of the Duchy of Brittany."

Francis answered, turning to Charles VII, "Monseigneur, I render you the same homage as have my predecessors and not a bit more."

After this, the two sovereigns walked about, chatting amiably. Charles was not a fighting monarch, nor was there here the personal enmity that developed two years later between Francis and Louis XI.

Louis XI was one of the cleverest kings in French history. Homely, with a fat figure and spindly legs, he dressed in a slovenly manner and was once mistaken for a peasant. To his contemporaries outside of France, however, he was known as the "Spider King," and many unfortunate political figures became enmeshed in his webs. He avoided war whenever possible, believing that "warfare is the most uncertain thing in the world," and "subtlety is always better than force." But when, without risking his person, he obtained a victim, he meted out punishments considered cruel even in an age accustomed to brutality.

When the Duke of Brittany went to render homage to Louis XI, the ceremony had been reduced to a mere formality. It would have been absurd to ask an oath of fidelity, for the Duke had already allied himself openly with all the enemies of France and had just signed a treaty with Charles the Bold of Burgundy. Louis had been informed of this by his spies, and Francis was aware that Louis knew of the treaty. Their hearts were full of hatred for each other, but their behavior remained courteous.

Though on the surface their relations were cordial, Louis was laying the groundwork for an invasion that would give him control of Brittany—a rich prize indeed. The following year, under the pretext of making a pilgrimage to the Abbey of Saint-Sauveur, he journeyed across Brittany to verify for himself what his informers had told him about the resources at Francis' disposal. The Duke was not deceived and took steps to counteract this espionage. He sent some of his followers, disguised as mendicant friars whose monks' habits inspired confidence, to arouse the people in Brittany, and other provinces as well, against the King of France. There were indeed French spies in Brittany, but there were also Breton spies in France!

During his long struggle with his powerful neighbor, Francis could trust no one. Many of the higher nobles were receiving bribes to support Louis against him when the time came for actual combat. Even his court favorite, though she was in love with Francis, was in the pay of the King of France! Louis was determined to add Brittany to the realms already subjugated by France, and when Anne was born he felt that fate was playing into his hands. He did not expect to have much trouble with the conquest when she became ruling duchess. He was counting, of course, on the hope that her father, now over forty, would not live long. However, it was Louis who died first—on April 30, 1483. Thus were passed on to his young son Charles and to his daughter Anne de Beaujeu the problems, hatreds, and ambitions concerning the annexation of Brittany.

Actual warfare had not yet broken out, although France had called up troops and Francis had ordered a general mobilization and arranged to have arms smuggled in from Italy with other merchandise. He found willing recruits, for the soldiers felt that they were going to fight to defend their country from invasion and to protect the little duchess whom they loved. They were especially loyal because the heir to the ducal throne was a girl and, in addition, bore the name of their patron saint.

Brittany had, at this time, a firm ally in England. Another ally, Austria, was sending troops from her dependent duchy, Flanders. Since, in addition to this power arrayed against them, the French also had Burgundy to contend with, the campaign against Brittany did not get started.

When the news of the death of Louis XI first reached

Nantes, the people turned out to celebrate. Surely now the danger of invasion was negligible. Charles VIII was only thirteen years of age, and his sister, who was now regent, was considered to be a flighty, foolish woman. Although Brittany's strong alliance with England was somewhat weakened by the sudden death of Edward IV and the consequent unrest in that country—Prince Edward, the rightful heir, had many enemies —this did not alarm the Bretons. Anne, even at the age of seven, had heard so much about King Louis, the great ogre, that she shared her father's violent hatred for their powerful enemy and was full of joy at the news of his death, believing, as did the people, that Brittany had now nothing to fear.

"Imagine, Isabeau," she cried to her sister as they danced around the fountain in the courtyard, "our father will be happier now, and *maman* will no longer worry about his going into danger in battle!"

"Yes," said Isabeau, "everything will be better now. And I'd be very happy, except that in a few years you will go away to marry the English prince and I shall never see you again!"

"Don't be silly!" chided her sister. "Of course we shall see each other. Why, maybe you will go with me!"

Isabeau brightened at that thought and impulsively threw her arms around her sister. "I do hope I may go with you! I should be so lonely without you that I think I would die!"

Anne hugged the too-thin body of her five-year-old sister close and wondered what it would be like to go far away to live in England.

But even at that moment, a ship was sailing from England with tragic news. The two little princes, Edward, to whom Anne was betrothed, and his brother Richard, had been mur-

dered in the Tower of London! It was said that guards had
crept in while the princes were sleeping and held pillows over
their faces until they died. By this act, the Earl of Gloucester,
uncle of the princes, became Richard III, King of England.
After he became king, England was no longer friendly toward
Brittany. The murder changed not only Anne's future but
the fate of her country.

Anne had never seen the boy who had been selected to be
her life companion, but she had heard him described as
charming and sweet-tempered—an ideal mate. She had grown
accustomed to the prospect of one day living in a foreign land,
perhaps as Queen of England. Now Edward was dead. The
story of his brutal murder shocked and saddened her. A
thoughtful child, mature for her age, she wondered what was
now in store for her. Since royal children were not safe from
their enemies, sometimes not even safe from ambitious relatives, what would be her fate? A new husband must now be
chosen for her—someone who would best serve the interests of
an independent Brittany. Royal children were betrothed or
even married in childhood to cement alliances between countries and had no control over their own destinies. Edward and
Anne had been merely pawns in a game played by their elders.

The common people of Brittany were wrong when they
thought their country was free of her enemies by reason of the
death of Louis XI. In fact, the real contest was just beginning.
In France there were many nobles—princes they were called—
who had resented the powerful rule of Louis. Upon his death,
with thirteen-year-old Charles as heir and his sister as regent,
they determined to get their revenge.

All his life, young Charles had lived at the Château d'Amboise. He had been kept a virtual prisoner there by his father, who did not provide any tutors to educate him. It was a large chateau and in 1483 it accommodated, in the old castle-keep, Anne de Beaujeu, her husband, and her brother-in-law, the Duke de Bourbon. Louis d'Orleans, heir presumptive to the crown, and several more lords occupied other parts of the chateau, and it was there, right under the nose of the regent, that all the ambitious princes of the blood met to discuss their plans for her overthrow.

The party of the princes, led by Louis d'Orleans, thought they could easily take over the reins of government, but they counted without the energy and ingenuity of Anne de Beaujeu, who was far wiser and cleverer than was generally thought. She was now determined to follow her father's policies toward Brittany. When this became clear, Francis knew that his best hope lay in getting as an ally the coalition of princes, so he sent an emissary to Louis d'Orleans to invite him to pay a visit to Nantes.

It was April, 1484. Louis arrived at Nantes, accompanied by the Count de Dunois and the Duke d'Alençon. All three were elegantly dressed young men—but Louis was the handsomest. His shoulder-length, light-brown hair curled slightly around a face that had strong features. He was twenty-two years old, gay, pleasure-loving, athletic, a good warrior, and a believer in whatever cause he lent his strength to. The cause at this time was a rallying of the French princes against the family of Beaujeu who showed the same determination as had Louis XI to keep the barons and princes out of power. He wanted, as did Francis of Brittany, to rescue young Charles from the influence of his sister.

A most cordial welcome was given Louis and his companions. At the formal dinner that was served upon their arrival, Francis introduced his daughter Anne, then eight years old. Her sister Isabeau was in bed with a fever.

"My daughter, dear cousin, is a most remarkable child," said Francis. "She astonishes even me with her proficiency in Latin and Greek."

Anne blushed as she made Louis a curtsy. "I have a most excellent tutor in Madame de Dinan," she replied. Her governess, who stood by, bowed and smiled.

"Ah, yes," commented Louis, returning the smile of Madame de Dinan, whom he knew. "I am aware that Madame is a very learned lady. And do you enjoy your studies?" he inquired of Anne, looking down from his six-foot height to the small figure in violet velvet.

"Yes, indeed, cousin. And I enjoy even more the romances in French that tell of deeds of heroism and chivalry." She darted a glance at Madame de Dinan, wondering if her governess guessed how much time was spent reading the lays of Chrétien de Troyes and Marie de France instead of studying.

"She reads everything in my library," the Duke said fondly. "It was not for nothing that I gathered so many art treasures and manuscripts from Italy, as well as more recent writings in the French tongue."

The visit of the French nobles, closely related by blood to Francis, was celebrated by a succession of fetes, banquets, tournaments, and balls. Anne, who was allowed to attend many of these events, admired her cousin Louis extravagantly. He seemed to her the personification of all the heroes she had read about. He was the kind of man about whom the minstrels sang. They had many long talks during his visit, and it amused him that she could converse in an adult manner even on topics of state. He realized that, in her, Francis had a worthy heir to the duchy. Louis particularly enjoyed their discussions of art and poetry, subjects about which, he was amazed to learn, she knew as much as he. But it was her winsome personality that remained in his memory. Louis was known as a ladies' man, but for many years he cherished in his heart the picture of the charming child in a violet velvet gown.

Flattered by all the attention she received from Louis, Anne faced his departure tearfully when, a few weeks later, after coming to an agreement with Francis in regard to opposing the Beaujeu faction with armed force, Louis and his companions took their leave. Mounted on richly caparisoned horses, the three nobles drew up in the courtyard before the little duchess. *"Adieu,* little cousin," Louis said.

"Not *adieu,* but *au revoir!"* cried Anne as she watched them ride away.

Louis turned and waved to the little figure dwarfed by the huge portal of the chateau. To his companions he remarked with feeling, "Eight years old and already an accomplished princess!"

The precocious princess continued to mature under the watchful tutelage of Madame de Dinan. She was never allowed to forget that she was heir to the duchy and would someday be its ruler. In her father's chateau, she had her own apartments and her own servants. Her half sister Françoise was her mistress of the wardrobe, and her half brother François was her knight-at-arms. She learned at an early age

to select ornaments, rich tapestries, and fine, carved furniture
for her reception room, her bedroom, and her oratory. She
showed much originality in decoration, and because she had
natural good taste, her rooms were not only beautiful, but
harmonious and restful, and always in them were books and
embroidery frames with work in progress. Madame de Dinan,
who had taught her all this without dominating her, was
proud of the result.

Anne, as she grew older, read or heard sung by visiting
minstrels many of the tales of chivalry of the medieval society
just ending. Knighthood was the aim of every boy who was
not a peasant. The lowly born might aspire to serve, but
could never dream of becoming one of the men in shining
armor whose deeds were sung before humble hearths as well
as in the halls of castles. Knights-at-arms were a part of every
king's household—and of every duke's—so it did not seem at
all strange to Anne that there should once have been a king
called Arthur, having at his Round Table a hundred knights
who spent their time righting wrongs or rescuing ladies from
scoundrels and vicious beasts. Knights, as in her father's court,
were still pledged to defend the honor of their lord or of any
lady who called on them for help. Anne, who dined with her
father and mother and a few favorites on a dais in a great hall,
below which stretched a long table that accommodated fifty
or sixty persons carefully placed according to rank, easily understood why Arthur, in his wisdom, had his table made
round. In that way, no knight might feel himself more important than another.

She knew the stories of Tristram and Iseult, Pelléas and
Mélisande, Aucassin and Nicolette—most of them sad stories,

though Aucassin and Nicolette lived happily ever after, and she was glad when she learned that. There were, too, the chronicles by Jean Froissart, which told of real events and people of the preceding century in France, England, Scotland, Belgium, and Italy. Many of these she read for herself in her father's library of manuscripts, but one in which she was particularly interested was told to her by her governess.

This chronicle described a siege and trial by combat which could still happen in her own city of Nantes in her own time. It had happened, however, a hundred years before at the Castle of Dinan, the ancestral home of her governess. Bertrand du Guesclin, a Breton, was one of the most popular leaders of his time. He won many battles during the Hundred Years' War with England and at one time defended the city of Rennes against an English attack.

"Tell me again, please, the story of the brave Bertrand," Anne would implore, and Madame de Dinan would gladly comply.

"As I have so often told you, dear one, in the year 1359, the Castle of Dinan, which was then newly built, was besieged by the English. No one could enter or leave the castle or the town. After the siege had continued for many months, those inside the castle were very hungry and the besiegers were very weary. So, though the English would not give up, they agreed to a truce of forty days. After the agreement was signed, the English could relax, and the Bretons could go out to get food and supplies.

"One day, Oliver, a knight who was brother to the great Bertrand du Guesclin, one of the commanders of the fortress, decided to take a ride on his horse outside the town. Had not the enemy agreed that anyone was free to go and come for forty days? But as he neared the outskirts, he was met by an English knight, Sir Thomas of Canterbury, who was accompanied by a few friends.

" 'Stop!' cried Sir Thomas. 'You are my prisoner!'

" 'Not so,' replied Oliver. 'There is a truce.'

" 'I care nothing for truces,' said Sir Thomas. 'Take him.' "

Anne broke in. "Oh, what a wicked man! I don't like him!"

"Yes, he was wicked not to observe the truce," said her governess. "Before Oliver could resist, the English surrounded him and pulled him from his horse. Forcing him to march ahead, they took him to Sir Thomas' tent, and there he was kept prisoner. And he was not gently used, I can assure you!

"Well, it was not long before Bertrand heard what had happened, for there had been witnesses. Besides, Oliver's horse had galloped off before he could be caught and had returned to Dinan without his master. Bertrand was furious. He mounted his horse, galloped furiously to the English camp, and demanded to see the Duke of Lancaster. Now, although there had been much fighting before the truce, there was politeness between the two warriors—as is the custom. The Duke, commander of the English forces, welcomed Bertrand and offered him some wine.

" 'Thank you, Your Grace,' said Bertrand, 'but I will not drink with you, for my brother Oliver has been unlawfully taken prisoner by one of your knights, Sir Thomas of Canterbury, and I come to demand his instant release.'

"The Duke of Lancaster, surprised at this, summoned Sir Thomas. He appeared, looking extremely arrogant. 'Does the Breton dare to imply that I have behaved in a manner un-

becoming to a knight?' he asked scornfully when the matter
had been explained. 'If so, let him prove it—by single combat.
Here is my glove!' And he threw his gauntlet at the feet of
Bertrand du Guesclin."

Again Anne broke in. "How did he dare when he knew he
was in the wrong?"

"Ah, my child," answered her governess, "there is always
one in a duel who dares even when he is in the wrong. But—
to the story. Bertrand quickly picked up the glove and cried,
'False knight, perjurer, and traitor! I will prove it on thy
body! I will fight thee before all the barons. And I swear by
the true God that I will not sleep in a bed nor break bread
until I have the right of thee in full armor at the point of the
sword!'

"The Duke, ashamed that one of his company should behave so badly, consented to the combat and even gave Bertrand a fine horse as a mark of his esteem. It was decided that
the duel should take place on the following day in the large
marketplace of Dinan with the Duke of Lancaster and the Sire
de Penhoen, Governor of Dinan, both present. The town was
to give hostages as evidence of good faith, and the Duke of
Lancaster was to be admitted with a train of a hundred
knights and barons.

"When the townspeople heard of the duel, they were filled
with fear. An enormous crowd pressed into the cathedral to
offer prayers for the success of their champion. Among them
was a lady, daughter of one of the richest inhabitants of Dinan,
who was famed for her learning in astrology and other occult
sciences. Typhaine Raguenel was her name, though she was

sometimes called 'Typhaine la Fée,' and it was rumored that she looked with particular favor on Bertrand du Guesclin.

" 'Do not be alarmed, good people,' she said to the crowd. 'Fear nothing for Bertrand, for he will be the victor in the conflict.' This comforted many of the people, but when her words were repeated to Bertrand, he said, 'Pay no heed to the words of a woman. I put my confidence in God and in my right.'

"As the time for the battle approached, Sir Thomas of Canterbury began to lose courage, so he sent a knight named Robert Knolles to attempt a reconciliation. But Bertrand was too angry. 'If he does not wish to fight,' he cried, 'let him give himself up to my mercy and present me with his sword, holding it by the point!'

" 'That he will not do,' said Knolles.

" 'He is right,' answered Bertrand. 'Honor is worth more than life.'

"At noon, the English duke and his barons, the Governor of Dinan, and a vast assemblage of townspeople, knights, and squires gathered in the marketplace to witness the combat. The trumpets sounded and, one from each side of the lists, the champions appeared. They were armed from head to foot and were riding horses covered with armor. It was a colorful scene, like all tournaments, but this was a duel in dead earnest, and honor was at stake.

"On a given signal, the combatants rode fiercely toward each other, and the lance of each of them shattered as it struck heavy armor plate. They returned to their places, then rode at each other again, swords unsheathed. The blows they gave struck fire from the steel armor, but no blood flowed. Again and again they assaulted each other, and the battle was long but with no advantage on either side. Finally, Bertrand seized hold of his adversary, and in the struggle Sir Thomas dropped his sword.

"With a cry, Bertrand sprang from his horse, grasped the sword, and threw it away from the lists. A great cheer went up from the Bretons. The Englishman then drove his horse against Bertrand to prevent his remounting, and he was hard put to it to avoid being crushed, impeded as he was by his heavy armor. But he managed to twist aside, and when Sir Thomas came at him again, Bertrand plunged his sword into the horse's flank, whereupon the horse reared and threw his rider. Before his adversary could recover himself, Bertrand seized him and struck him repeatedly with his mailed fist.

" 'Cease and desist!' cried the Duke of Lancaster. 'It is enough!'

"Then Robert Knolles cried out, 'My Lord Duke, I beg that Bertrand du Guesclin grant Sir Thomas his life, if it be your pleasure.'

" 'What say you?' asked the Duke, addressing Bertrand.

" 'I grant him his life, as the Duke sees fit,' answered Bertrand.

" 'You have fought valiantly,' the Duke said. 'Your brother will be restored to you, and I will give him a thousand livres. And this knight will come no more to my court.'

"Well, that is the way it turned out," Madame de Dinan said, concluding the story. "Lancaster returned to his camp with his followers, Oliver was restored to his brother, and the day ended with a grand fete celebrated by the inhabitants in honor of Bertrand. The beautiful Typhaine was present at the fete. Bertrand soon began to court the lady, and it was not long before they were married at Pontorson, of which he was then governor. They lived happily ever after and often gazed from their castle across the waters between them and Mont-Saint-Michel with its chapel topped by the towering statue of the saint. When the valiant Bertrand died, his heart was buried beside his wife, who had not lived as long as he, in the church of the Jacobins at Dinan."

"Oh," cried Anne, "what a romantic tale! And how fitting that they who had lived so happily together should not be divided in death! His heart, at least, rested beside hers." Although she was only a child, Anne's mind had been so conditioned to the prevailing ideas of honor as an attribute of chivalry that she could understand the story of Bertrand du Guesclin—and even the custom, still followed in her day, of removing the heart of a hero or sovereign when he died in order to place it in a position of importance or sentiment.

Surrounded by the wild beauty of the landscape and the cultivated beauty of the palace, her mind well educated in the culture of the Greeks and Romans, and her imagination fed by tales of folklore and romance, eight-year-old Anne had attained a knowledge of her world and her people not reached today by young people until they are well into their teens. Life was simple, knowledge was scanty, religion explicit, and little time was devoted to play. When one's life expectancy was only twenty-five years, there was no time to waste, especially for a duchess, and stirring events were taking place in France and Brittany that were to shape Anne's future.

CHAPTER III

Defeat and Death

LIKE ALL SOVEREIGNS of his time, Francis II maintained a huge court of retainers who lived at his expense. Some were sincerely helpful; others mere parasites who gave him only flattery. He had favorites, not only among the ladies, but among the men. Many of his courtiers were relatives—children with titles could be married only to someone of their own rank, so nearly all were cousins in some degree. The Marshal de Rieux, a tutor of Anne's, Alain d'Albret, half brother of Madame de Dinan, and Philippe de Montauban were some of those upon whom Francis depended. The Duke was apt to be too trusting in his relations with his officials and suffered thereby.

There was one young man of lowly birth who came to the palace as the servant of the Duke's tailor. The Duke took a fancy to this servant and made him Master of the Wardrobe. Unlike most of his class, Pierre Landais could read and write proficiently, and he soon gained a position of authority in the

Duke's household. He became Minister of Finance, then Counsellor of War, then head of the Navy and the Police. He was efficient in all his offices and contributed greatly to the prosperity of Brittany. Finally, he was named Prime Minister of the Privy Council. Of course he made many enemies on his way up. Francis' relatives were horrified at the sudden rise to power of this interloper and at the influence he had over the Duke. Even the common people hated him because, though one of themselves, he had power over them which they were willing to concede only to someone born to high rank.

Landais made himself secure with the Duke's favorite by giving her money and praise. When she died, he resolved to be the only power over Francis. To do this, he had to get rid of the Chancellor, Guy Chauvin—a man of integrity who could not easily be deceived. Landais made up a false charge against the Chancellor and got permission from Francis to arrest him. Without trial, Chauvin was imprisoned and his property confiscated, and his wife and children were left to starve. He was sent from the dungeons of Nantes to Auray and then to l'Ermine—each time to worse conditions and more cruel jailors, until he died of misery and starvation. Because of this and other acts of tyranny, the Breton nobles united against Landais and sought him out in the chateau with the intention of killing him. He managed to escape them, and his master protected him on the grounds that he was indispensable to the government of the realm.

By the time Anne was seven, it was Pierre Landais who was negotiating with foreign powers. Francis had grown weary. The constant conflicts of his reign, the need to be continually making alliances with one foreign prince against another, the physical strain and intrigue had tired him, and he depended more and more on Landais—to the consternation of the other members of the council. It was Landais who made the treaty with Maximilian of Austria and Richard III of England for the avowed purpose of guaranteeing the independence of Brittany and the weakening of France. Anne de Beaujeu knew of all this through her spies. To counter these moves, she made an alliance with Flanders to support France against Austria. She spent money with a lavish hand, giving bribes to the nobles who were jealous of Landais and to many among the populace who had suffered from his harshness and his arrogance.

Nevertheless, there were those who supported Landais and what he represented as head of the government. These supporters desired to keep Brittany free, and Landais was able to gather together an army to fight against France. But because of the bribes they had received, many of the Breton nobles and their retainers declared themselves on the side of France. Brittany was a country divided. Landais knew this state of affairs would be disastrous, so in the month of June, 1485, he sent the army, commanded by Anne's half brother, François d'Avaugour, south of Rennes to meet and defeat the army of the rebel nobles. There they engaged in what came to be known as the "Silly War."

With pennants flying, the two armies met in a flowering meadow on a sunny June day, each drawn up in battle array with bowmen and horsemen. There they stared at each other, near enough to recognize friends, relatives, men from the same village. The longer they stared, the harder it became for their commanders to give the order to charge.

An aide-de-camp whispered to his colonel, "Look, Mon-seigneur, it is your cousin who commands the right flank. Do you wish to see him killed?"

"It is true that he has not remained loyal to the govern-ment," answered the colonel, "but I should not wish him to be killed."

"My brother is among the rebels," said the aide. "We quar-reled over his decision to support France, but I cannot raise a weapon against him."

The whispers grew to murmurs among the men and com-manders on each side, and soldiers shifted positions to get a better view of the individuals in the opposing formation, until where there had been two armies, there now was simply an assemblage of men-at-arms loath to go ahead with the battle.

Finally, an emissary under a flag of truce was sent galloping from the loyal side to the rebels. He saluted their commander and asked for a conference of the leaders in the name of the Sire d'Avaugour. Pierre Landais, not being a soldier, was at a safe post in the castle, from which he had given the com-mand to the army to wipe out the rebels.

The leaders withdrew to a nearby knoll where a green silk tent was set up for their conference. Meanwhile a bowman saw his next-door neighbor in the front rank of the opposing archers and ran over to greet him. A knight rode across the greensward to talk to his cousin, and there were tears and embraces. Others followed suit, and finally, being tired, they all sat down in complete amity and awaited the outcome of the conference. It was an amazing sight—the two armies in-termingled, their pennants drooping! A bottle of wine was produced here and there, and talk and laughter became general. Some knights were more reserved, knowing that it was possible that hostilities might be begun, and these walked their horses restlessly around the edge of the army that had turned out to be just a crowd of men.

In the tent, the leaders talked a long time. Why had some of the nobles decided to support France against their own land of Brittany after all these centuries of independence so dear to their hearts? Did they not know that Louis d'Orleans was the head of a coalition that would fight on their side against the regent of France? The fact that French money had been an influence was not mentioned. The real cause of the split, they suddenly realized, was Francis' minister, Pierre Landais. He was to blame for everything. How could a man no better than a peasant have gained such power! Who was he to tell them—nobles, princes of the blood—what to do! They had failed to get rid of him once; there must be no failure a second time. When all this had been discussed and the rebel lords had been asked if they would now change and swear allegiance to Francis, one of them stood up and shouted:

"Vive François, Duc de Bretagne! A bas Pierre Landais!"

A cheer went up. Yes, they would support Francis, their rightful lord, but down with Landais! He must be removed. And soon the cry changed to *"Mort à Landais, mort à Landais!"* Only by his death could they curtail his power. They had met on a battlefield and come close to killing one another, all because of Landais. Only his death would satisfy them.

As the setting sun tinged the assembled ranks with a soft rose color, the commanders filed out of the green silk tent and the message went forth: "Peace and concord. We fight for Francis and Brittany. We are united against France." So all went home, and that was the end of the "Silly War."

When the leaders reached Nantes, they sought an audience with the Duke. During the conference, Francis was heard to cry out, "No, I cannot! He is my friend! Do not try to persuade me, my lords. I will never give the order for his execution!"

"But, Monseigneur," one of the generals said vehemently, "give us leave to seize him. He is hiding in the palace. Let us seek him out."

Francis, alarmed, dismissed the petitioners. "Leave at once," he cried. "I forbid you to search the chateau!"

When the committee left the castle, the square was filled with people shouting their demand that Landais be given up to them. The soldiers had spread the word and the populace was enraged. Francis sent for his brother-in-law, the Count de Foix, to appease them. After appearing on one of the balconies to talk to the crowd, he returned to the Duke.

"I would rather be prince over a thousand wild boars than over such a people as these Bretons," he said. "You must give Landais up to them, or you are lost."

It was perhaps a just retribution for the cruel Landais that it was the Chancellor, the successor to Chauvin, who came to the ducal hall to arrest him.

"Why do my people want you to arrest him?" asked the Duke sorrowfully.

"Because grave charges are hanging over him," answered the Chancellor.

"Promise me that only justice will be done," said the Duke.

"That I promise you, Monseigneur."

Francis drew the trembling Landais from his hiding place behind a tapestry that hung in back of the Duke's chair of state. "I give him to you most reluctantly," Francis said, "and I command you again that he receive justice."

Pierre Landais was conducted to the prison in the tower of Nantes. His trial was not delayed, and the crimes of which he was held guilty were not difficult to prove. The Duke did not attend the trial and was greatly worried as to its outcome. He was informed that the council would report to him at the end of the trial and would act as he commanded.

"Then," said the Duke, "whatever Landais has done, I will grant him pardon. I do not wish him to die."

However, on the very next day, July 20, 1485, a huge gathering assembled before the castle where a gibbet had been erected, and at noon the unfortunate Landais, bound and divested of his clothes of office, was led out. As a roar went up from the crowd, Anne and Isabeau went to a window to see what was causing the disturbance.

"Oh," cried Anne, "it is Monsieur Landais!"

Madame de Dinan called out to her, "Do not look, my child! He has been an enemy to Brittany, and so he must die."

"My father has not thought so," countered Anne.

"But it has been proved at his trial," said her governess. "And see—your father is not there. He does not prevent it."

"That is true," said Anne slowly. "And if Landais is an enemy to Brittany, he should die! I shall look."

She watched the execution without flinching, and the spirit within her hardened to the thought that her country must

come first—everyone who was not good for it must die. But
Isabeau covered her ears against the shrieks of the mob and
lay, sobbing, on her cushion.

When the death of Landais was reported to the Duke,
Francis wept and ordered that his friend be honorably buried.
Feeling feeble and remorseful, Francis had no ambition to
pursue the war against France.

Ever since the death of the little English prince to whom
Anne had been betrothed, Francis had been striving to use
the promise of his daughter's hand in marriage as a means of
cementing his alliance with some foreign country, or even of
assuring the loyalty of his own nobles. Most of these matri-
monial negotiations were carried on by messengers so that
there would be nothing on paper that might cause Francis
embarrassment later. He held out this bait to the Duke of
Buckingham in England, to the heir to the Spanish throne,
to Maximilian of Austria, and, in his own country, to the
Viscount de Rohan and Alain d'Albret. Anne, with a dowry
of the whole province of Brittany, was a negotiable asset, and
Francis, driven by fear and fatigue, was trying to make the
most of it and to avoid war. This he was able to do for a time.

Richard III of England had now been supplanted by Henry
of Lancaster, who was friendly to Anne de Beaujeu, so Louis
d'Orleans was forced to disband his followers and wait for a
more auspicious time to take up arms against the regency in
France.

During the interval of peace, two sad events affected the
lives of Anne and Isabeau. Marguerite de Foix, their mother,
closed her eyes for the last time. She had been devoted to

them, and the children indeed loved her very much. Though
they spent much of their time with their nurse or governess,
they were always happy when *maman* stayed with them for a
while, or when they were allowed to watch the parties and
fetes that made up a large part of the palace life. Their mother
appeared to them to be the most beautiful of all the ladies,
though often she looked sad. Her passing meant real grief—
the first that Anne had known. She was saddened by the
thought that life was brief and, she was beginning to see, not
always happy.

Soon after her mother died, Anne's half brother Antoine,
who was so mischievous and whom everybody loved, fell ill
with a fever which ended his short life at the age of eight. The
sisters missed his liveliness and his pranks, though otherwise
life went on much as usual.

Anne's thoughts turned ever more constantly to religion,
which was always to be a vital part of her life. The colorful
pageantry of the medieval church and the daily Masses in the
chateau chapel had a deep significance for her. She was naturally devout, and had she not been heir to a ducal throne, she
would probably have become a nun. Did she not bear the
name of Saint Anne—Saint Anne, who was the mother of the
Virgin Mary and the grandmother of Jesus of Nazareth? The
legends about the saint made Anne long to be worthy of her
name, and she resolved at an early age that if she became
duchess in truth, with the power her father had, she would
rule her people kindly and devote much of the kingdom's
revenue to the church and to the poor. But, even so, she would
rule with a firm hand. Her country must come first, and any
like Pierre Landais who would disrupt the unity of the king-

dom would be punished. She did not intend to be a weak sovereign.

In 1486, the coalition of French princes reunited to make plans for the overthrow of the regency. At this time, the court of France was at the Château d'Amboise—after the death of Louis XI, a host of officials and retainers had moved there to wait upon Charles VIII. And it was there that the princes of the blood again met with Louis d'Orleans to curtail the power of Anne de Beaujeu.

After they had made their new plans, Louis d'Orleans paid another visit to Nantes to confer with Francis II. He was amazed to see how the Duke had failed since the execution of Pierre Landais. Francis seemed subdued and weary, but his council welcomed an alliance with the princes, and he agreed that something must be done soon. Letters were sent to England, and because that country was once more unfriendly toward France, several battalions were promised in support of Brittany. Austria, too, promised aid, and it appeared that the coalition now had a good chance of success.

Louis saw Anne again at this time. How she had grown! he thought. Ten years old, she had begun to take on the airs of a duchess—a little more sure of herself, a little imperious. Her mother was gone now, and Anne apparently felt that she must take her place.

Anne was glad to see Louis and thought him more charming than ever. "Will there be a battle soon to drive the wicked French from our boundaries?" she asked him.

"Soon, I think, cousin, and may the victory be ours!"

"I know you will lead, and I fear you will be in great danger!"

"There is always danger in battle, *ma petite.*" He smiled down at her, for though she was taller than she had been at eight years old, she was still under five feet and he towered above her. "But never fear—I shall come out of it unscathed!"

She did not cry when he left this time, but smiled her farewell, and later prayed earnestly for his safety in the battle.

That battle was further off than Louis had thought. It took a long time to marshal troops from a foreign country, and without them, the princes did not dare to go ahead. Travel was slow—the soldiers from Austria had to march on foot across Europe, and there were many hazards on the way.

Most of these hazards were the result of the efforts of Anne de Beaujeu, determined to prevent foreign aid from reaching the coalition. Through her agents, she managed to stir up a rebellion in Flanders, which was under the control of Austria. While leading his troops against the insurrectionists, Maximilian, the Austrian duke, was captured and held in prison for four months before he succeeded in buying his freedom. The French barons who were in sympathy with the coalition were ferreted out, and any against whom there was the least suspicion of disloyalty were seized.

Time dragged on, and in late 1487, the French pushed a campaign against Brittany that succeeded in weakening the border armies. Finally, in July of 1488, the French army, under the command of the famous General La Tremouille, met in a pitched battle with the forces of the confederates— the princes of the coalition, the Breton divisions, the Austrian contingents, and the English battalions—at Saint-Aubin-du-Cormier on Breton soil. It was a short but furious battle, and victory went to the French. The gallant Louis d'Orleans was captured and imprisoned. When the news of the defeat reached Francis, the Duke was disheartened and at the end of his resources—he had been obliged for many months to feed and pay foreign mercenaries as well as his own troops. He sent emissaries to the court of France to sue for peace.

It was a sad day for the Bretons, and Francis, feeling that things were hopeless, decided to have a talk with his daughter. She came at his summons and made her usual grave curtsy.

"My daughter," he began, "you are now twelve years old, and I think it will not be long before you are reigning duchess of our poor Brittany."

"Oh, don't say that, *papa!*" cried Anne. "It makes me feel so sad."

"I do not wish to alarm you, but I must warn you—I have to prepare you for what must inevitably come. I have devoted my entire life to preserving the independence of Brittany and hoped that I might hand down to you a prosperous and free country. I have failed. Perhaps you will do better. But there are dangers to be faced, and when I die . . ."

"Ah, *papa*—do not speak of that!"

"It must be spoken of, Anne. There will be many suitors for your hand, all bent on capturing for himself and his province the homeland we both love. Choose wisely, *ma petite* —choose the one who will best preserve the prosperity and integrity of Brittany!"

Anne straightened her shoulders and held her head high. "When I am Duchess of Brittany," she said, "I will do my best—and always what I think you would wish. But, oh, let us *not* talk of death!"

"You are right," Francis answered, "and I cannot talk of

independence for Brittany until I know what terms of peace will be granted us now." He sighed. "I fear France, under that woman, will not be generous!"

He was right, and the terms of peace were hard indeed. Anne de Beaujeu demanded that Francis II give up his throne, that his daughters be married to French barons of proved loyalty, and that Brittany be attached to the kingdom of France.

At the announcement of these terms, young Charles VIII stepped forth and demanded his prerogative. After all, he was King of France, though for so long as a minor that his wishes had never been consulted. Now he was eighteen, and his kindly nature made him wish to be generous. He said—and his chancellor, Guillaume de Rochefort, agreed with him— that the penalties demanded by his sister were of the sort exacted by Alexander the Great or Julius Caesar—pagan leaders who knew nothing of Christianity. Charles was filled with chivalric ideals and believed that Brittany should be more gently treated so that its people might become willing allies of France.

And so the Treaty of Verger was drawn up, leaving Francis his title, but with provisions that would make it difficult for Brittany ever to take arms against France in the future. The treaty stipulated that all foreign troops should be sent home and that Brittany must never again call on them to aid her. Furthermore, Francis must agree to consult and gain the consent of France to the chosen husband before the marriage of either of his daughters. To assure compliance with these provisions, the Duke of Brittany must pledge the great seals of the council, the church, the *seigneuries,* and the cities. If he broke

faith, a fine of 200,000 *écus* of gold would be levied against
the large cities. In return, France agreed to evacuate Brittany,
with the exception of garrisons in St. Malo, Dinan, Fougères,
and Saint-Alban, which would be left until such time as the
French deemed it safe to withdraw. And if the Duke's daughters married without the consent of France, those four cities
would become French territory. In addition to all this, Francis
must render homage to the King of France and obey the
Parliament in Paris.

The terms of the treaty were only a little less severe than
those prepared by Anne de Beaujeu, but they did, at least,
leave Francis his dignity. That, however, was not enough for
him. Anne watched her father's health fail day by day. It was
now clear to all that Francis had not long to live. He did not
want any dispute over the succession, so he sent couriers to
summon the most important nobles to attend him at Nantes.
There, with her invalid father propped up by cushions in a
chair beside her, Anne sat in the seat of state and received the
oath of allegiance from her most influential subjects.

Francis did not appoint a regent for his daughter, but instead formed a council to advise her. He named, first of all,
Philippe de Montauban, his loyal chancellor; then the Marshal de Rieux and Madame de Dinan, who had each had a
hand in her education; and after them, three important
nobles—Alain d'Albret, the Count de Dunois, and the Duke
de Comminges.

When the plague broke out at Nantes, Francis and his
daughters, courtiers, and servants traveled to nearby Coiron
—a small chateau on the Loire River. It was with a sad heart
that Francis looked back at his castle in Nantes, a symbol in its

strength and beauty of all he had wanted for Brittany. "I think that I shall not see it again," he said.

When they arrived at Coiron, Francis took to his bed. "I have tried and I have failed," he said. "I have not the heart to try another time."

Three weeks later, he died.

CHAPTER IV

The Only Way Out

IMMEDIATELY AFTER THE FUNERAL of Francis II, Duke of Brittany, Anne, Isabeau, and the courtiers traveled to another, more strongly fortified chateau at Guérande, which was considered a safer place for the young Duchess. During the twelve years that Nantes had been her home, Anne and all the court had at times been obliged to leave it—often for a month or more. Sometimes it was because the plague had broken out there, as had recently happened. This pestilence, which was named the Black Death, had been known to Europe ever since 1348, when it had swept away one-third of the entire population. Because the terrifying disease struck the highborn as well as the peasant, spread so rapidly, and killed its victims in a matter of hours, everyone who was able to get away fled whenever a fresh outbreak occurred. Sometimes, however, the Duke and his court left Nantes out of fear of a surprise attack, for this city was close to the southern boundary of Brittany. On one occasion, when it was thought that danger threatened them, Philippe de Montauban had taken the two sleeping princesses in his arms and galloped away on his fastest horse.

For the last year, the French armies had stayed very near, a constant menace. Strongly fortified though it was, and perhaps impregnable, the great castle which sheltered the ducal household might be subjected to a siege. Most sieges were successful, and such a maneuver would quickly end the resistance of the Bretons and mean their immediate conquest by their powerful neighbor.

The little girls did not mind traveling about. There were many beautiful, if smaller, chateaux in the country that they enjoyed visiting. Besides men-at-arms and throngs of servants, much household equipment accompanied them. A long procession of mules carried their beds, the chairs reserved for them alone, clothing, bedding, china, silver, and cooking utensils. Often, if the weather was good, the trips were very pleasant. But this occasion was different—both daughters were sad because of their father's death, but Anne was particularly troubled. Ever since infancy, she had been schooled to meet this situation, yet now that the time had come, she was tormented by doubts and fears. On her alone rested the decision that would determine the future of her beloved Brittany, for she would be obliged to marry—not at some time in the future, but very, very soon.

Of course, her choice would not be made without a great deal of advice and a great deal of pressure, though she did not dream now of how many friends and supporters would be lost to her in the process. She knew that her marriage would be a political one, for her dowry of the whole province of Brittany was a rich one indeed for the successful suitor—and, naturally, her council would expect to arrange the matter. She could not hope, like an ordinary girl, to please herself in choosing a husband. She was aware that, of those eligible, she must select the man who could do the most toward preserving the independence of her country. And yet, by the Treaty of Verger, this husband must first meet with the approval of the King of France. How this could be managed, she couldn't see, but it was not long before she realized that the members of her council did not intend the Treaty of Verger to stand in the way of Breton ambition.

Her advisors behaved politely toward each other in the council meetings, but Anne began to sense that there was disunity among them, though she did not yet know just how they were divided. Philippe de Montauban was her strong friend and adviser, but she saw that Madame de Dinan and the Marshal de Rieux resented her attempt to be the head of the government. When she used the royal "we" in her council meetings, they clucked behind their hands. When she asked for a statement of the financial situation of her country, they came out openly against the discussion of such matters before a mere child. In their eyes, she was still their pupil and any attempt to take over the reins of government was dangerous to them—for they had plans. But Anne pretended not to notice and demanded to know the facts. The Chancellor, of course, had all the facts, and he proceeded to enlighten her on the sad state of Brittany's finances. Other pertinent questions asked by the new Duchess were so astute, so penetrating that Madame de Dinan wondered if she had not gone too far in her education of her pupil and wished either that she had done her work less well or that the little Duchess had not been so apt a student. Philippe de Montauban, seeing their discomfiture, smiled to himself. He intended to do everything in his power to advise and protect the young ruler who showed such an independent spirit.

The only subject the council seemed united on was opposition to France. In less than two weeks after their arrival at Guérande, an ambassador arrived from the court of France. Clothed in yellow and purple velvet and riding a horse richly caparisoned, he was followed by six men-at-arms and a dozen lackeys and grooms. His entrance into the courtyard of the small chateau was impressive. Anne received him as she sat at a table presiding over her council. A thick cushion in her chair of state gave her added height. In spite of her youth and her small stature, her bearing was dignified, even regal, but in her heart were misgivings. She knew well the danger from these Frenchmen! Her father was dead and her cousin, Louis d'Orleans, who would have been her protector and friend, was far away in prison, captive of this same enemy. Her southern and eastern borders were in peril. What ultimatum could she expect now?

The ambassador's words were courteous, his bows and flourishes most polite, and the menace hidden in his message did not appear until the very end. First of all, he expressed, on behalf of the French king, Charles VIII, and his sister, Anne de Beaujeu, great sorrow over the death of their dear friend and cousin, Francis of Brittany. They were aware of what a heavy burden of affairs had fallen upon such young shoulders as hers, and they wished to be of assistance. Settling the weighty matters of state that confronted the little Duchess would, no doubt, take a long time, and so the King of France desired that the two princesses, Anne and Isabeau, should be placed under his protection and—the ambassador hesitated before adding the final blow—the King thought it best that he should have control of the administration of the duchy as well! This, of course, was not according to the agreement that Francis had signed; it was asking for the prize of conquest without fighting for it.

Anne looked at her council, whose rights were being so arrogantly passed over, and read the anger in their faces. She spoke haughtily. "Monsieur, does not the King of France remember that there is a treaty between our two countries—the Treaty of Verger?" she asked the ambassador.

"I am sure he does, Your Grace," he replied.

"Thank him for us for his kind offer of assistance," said the Duchess Anne with dignity, "and tell him that messengers will be sent to his court with our answer in due time."

"But meanwhile, Your Grace is in great danger . . ." began the ambassador.

"In great danger," said Anne firmly. "A danger that I shall attempt to forestall."

The ambassador, surprised at being so quickly reprimanded by a mere child, started to protest, but as he looked at the grim countenances of the members of her council, he thought better of it, bowed, and withdrew.

After a suitable interval, Anne sent messengers to Charles VIII, reminding him that by the Treaty of Verger, Brittany was to be left free of French control if the other provisions of the treaty were adhered to. She stated further that she intended to keep her part of the bargain, but would make no concessions other than those already agreed to by her dead father.

This answer, stemming from her heart, was a clever repudiation of French greed, but Anne de Beaujeu, still controlling the policy of her young brother, was quick to adopt a more devious way to satisfy her ambition. Her plan involved one of the more powerful barons of Brittany, the Viscount de Rohan. Because of her effective spy system, all that happened in Brittany was known to the French court. It was known, for instance, that of the several suitors for the hand of the young Duchess, the first to press his intentions was this same Viscount de Rohan. A middle-aged man, he did not ask that he himself should be her husband, but he proposed that his two sons should marry the two princesses, Anne and Isabeau. These two boys were much younger than Anne, and she could not imagine herself married to either of them. There had been another son, older than Anne, for whom she had had cousinly affection, but he had been killed in the battle of Saint-Aubin-du-Cormier. She was not impressed by the Viscount's claim to be directly descended from Count Meriadec, the first King of Brittany, and she was alarmed by his boast that he would fight any and all who opposed his wishes.

The council was not willing to agree to his plans for the princesses, nor were many barons, who did not want to see Rohan gain power in this way. They accepted his challenge, and he opposed them with his personal army. A small war began, with French battle units fighting beside those of the Viscount. Eventually there were more French forces involved than those of Rohan, and when the cities of Morlaix and Concarneau were captured and finally the large seaport of Brest, it became evident to the Viscount that these cities were not in his possession but in the hands of the French. He had been their tool! Anne de Beaujeu had been playing the game that her father, Louis XI, had found so successful; thanks to her pretended support of Rohan, there was civil war in Brittany, which might soon serve as an excuse for France to step in as an intermediary.

All this took many months. The Duchess Anne was sad to see her country so divided. Her council was fearful that if the conquests by the French should continue, Anne would be forced to marry some French prince, and Brittany would be immediately annexed. For some time they had been negotiating with Henry VII of England, pleading for help against France. It was not very hard to convince the King that England's ancient enemy would be far more powerful if she held also the great province of Brittany. Eventually Henry made an agreement with the little Duchess whereby England would immediately dispatch ten thousand soldiers for her defense if, in return, she would later relinquish to him one of the Breton cities now in French hands. England still claimed part of the continent and still had visions of reconquering France.

This treaty was heartening to Anne's council, but it took months to conclude. Messengers rode on horseback to a nearby port, embarked in a sailing vessel for England, and once there, took horse again for the hundred-mile journey to London. Henry's messengers had the same trip in reverse. And troops sent by him to Brittany would have the same long journey, much lengthened because the archers and other foot soldiers would have to cover the land distances by marching. In the meantime, Anne was being besieged by suitors and those who tried to influence her in behalf of one or the other. Besides the sons of the Viscount de Rohan, there were three principal suitors for her hand: Alain, Sire d'Albret, the half brother of Madame de Dinan; Jean de Chalons, Prince d'Orange—both Bretons—and from faraway Austria, Duke Maximilian, recently crowned King of the Romans. The second of these had a really formidable obstacle in his way—he was already married! Although divorce was not countenanced in those days, an annulment could be obtained by special dispensation of the Pope, but such termination of a marriage took many months to conclude and was very costly. For this reason, time worked against the Prince d'Orange, and he could hardly expect to be available when the Duchess made her choice.

Alain d'Albret was a widower. He was fifty years old, had an ugly, twisted body, a red pockmarked face, a ferocious expression, a raucous voice, and was already the father of seven children. Anne could not bear to look at him, and the thought of marriage with him nauseated her. She realized that she must make some sacrifice, but this she would not do! Yet it was to this union that her lifelong friend, cousin, and governess, Madame de Dinan, expected her to agree. She was blinded to Anne's feelings by her own greed and ambition. Day after day, she urged the young Duchess to agree to marry Albret, and day after day, Anne refused even to consider the matter.

"But Madame! How can you expect me to marry someone who is so repugnant to me?"

"You must overcome your personal feelings for the good of

your country. Do you not see that marriage with such a powerful baron would make Brittany safe from the French?"

"No, I do not see it! We would still be at war with France
and we might easily lose. Besides, I cannot bear to think of it!"

"Remember all I have done for you, all I have taught you.
Does that not merit a reward? Your marriage to my half
brother would greatly elevate my position."

"Ah, cousin, I should not like to appear ungrateful, but
this man fills me with disgust! I will not do as you ask."

"If you cannot be persuaded, I can use other means."

"I do not know what you are threatening, but nothing could
be worse than what you wish me to do!"

Conversations of this sort went on for months. Madame did
not cease to persuade and threaten, and Anne continued to
refuse. The strain was affecting her health. To whom could
she turn? Her little sister was too young to offer advice, but
the two girls could discuss the suitors and often did. One day
as they talked, Isabeau was lying down—she was frailer than
ever now—and Anne had her arms around her, holding her
close.

"Isabeau, darling, the time is drawing near when I shall not
be able to put off any longer my choice of a husband. I must
talk about it, for I can think of nothing else!"

"Oh, Anne, what a pity that Prince Edward was murdered!
You might be married to him now. From all we heard, he was
a fine, handsome youth. And he was young!"

"Alas, yes! But he is dead, and I must choose one of the
suitors."

"The Viscount de Rohan's sons, Jacques and Jean, are not

suitors now, are they, since their father is fighting with the French against us?"

"I suppose not. Yet if the French win more of our territory, they may force me to marry one of them, or a French prince—which would be worse!"

"If only the Viscount's son François had not been killed in battle! We both liked him."

"Yes, I liked François, but Jacques and Jean are only babies. I want a husband who will be my equal and help me rule Brittany."

"And the Prince d'Orange cannot marry now. He is at least a gentleman," Isabeau said. "That leaves only that horrible Alain d'Albret!"

"You have forgotten that messengers have come from the court of Maximilian of Austria asking the honor of my hand in marriage."

"That's true," said Isabeau. "What kind of man is he?"

"I know very little about him. He is a widower over thirty years old, and has a little daughter who is betrothed to Charles of France and lives at the French court. But he is said to be brave and honorable and is the head of a very wealthy kingdom. His wealth would help Brittany."

"He cannot be worse than Monsieur d'Albret," said Isabeau with a shudder. "Whatever happens, I hope you may not have to marry *him!*"

"That is the way I feel," Anne said. "But my council wants me to marry a Breton noble. Oh, it is very hard to be a woman and the head of a state! If I were a man, I could do as I pleased!"

And in calling herself a woman, Anne was right. Always

precocious, she had been further matured by the struggle and responsibility of the last year. She was nearly fourteen and must make mature decisions important to the duchy. She was indeed a woman!

When Madame de Dinan decided that persuasion had failed, she at last fulfilled her threat to use other means. She secured the support of the Marshal de Rieux, one of Anne's guardians, and in the name of the government of Brittany a message was sent to the Pope in Rome, informing His Holiness that there existed a document written by Francis II of Brittany and signed by his daughter Anne stating that she would marry the Sire d'Albret. Because they were cousins—though not first cousins—the government respectfully requested the papal blessing on this union. At the same time, Alain d'Albret sent a similar message to His Holiness, and without even waiting for an answer from the Pope, the betrothal was announced. Anne knew that her danger was immediate, and she sought the advice of her Chancellor, Philippe de Montauban, her staunchest ally.

The document was produced, and though Anne did not remember it, she recognized her childish signature. How had her father ever had such an agreement drawn up! But it had indeed been signed by her some years before. Acting on the advice of Montauban, Anne asked for a convocation of the Ecclesiastical Council. To this solemn body, she declared that she did not now and never had knowingly consented to a marriage with Alain d'Albret and, though it appeared that she had signed the document when she was ten years old, she had not understood its import and had signed merely to please her dear father, now dead. She had her protest formally registered and sent word of her action to the Sire d'Albret and the Marshal de Rieux. She now considered the latter her enemy.

The surprise maneuver executed by Madame de Dinan and Rieux split Anne's advisory council into two hostile groups. Montauban, Dunois, and Comminges remained loyal to her. Knowing her danger if she remained in the palace, Anne and her court, accompanied by Philippe de Montauban and a troop of mercenary soldiers under the command of the Count de Dunois, left Guérande for Redon. Rieux, who was supposed to be her protector, headed a revolt against her and installed himself, together with Alain d'Albret and Madame de Dinan, in the city of Nantes, which he had seized by force of arms. Thus, in addition to the encroachment of an enemy who had captured several of her southern cities, Brittany was again faced with civil war. Most of the people were loyal to their little Duchess, but Rieux had an army. After reviewing the situation, Anne's Chancellor advised that she go to Nantes and demand the return of that city to her, the rightful sovereign.

On a dreary winter day, when the sky, thick with black clouds, seemed to mirror the unhappy plight of her country, Anne set out—accompanied by two of her faithful barons, their escort, and a small troop of bowmen—to reclaim the city and the castle that had been her home. At La Paquelaie, three leagues distant from Nantes, she halted the procession and sent messengers ahead to demand that the gates be opened.

After the messengers had departed, Anne and Montauban rode their horses to a little mound from which they could see the Château de Nantes, towering high above the beautiful Loire River. Even from this distance, she could see the bastion whose smooth stone rose forty feet above the river and on which, she knew, was planted the little garden where she and Isabeau used to play. Above it, from the grim round towers which guarded the citadel, pennants were flying. They would not now be blazoned with the ermine of Brittany, she realized, but with the coat of arms of the Marshal de Rieux. She wondered if she was ever again to live in the home of her childhood.

When her message was received, Alain d'Albret and his followers left Nantes to intercept the Duchess at La Paquelaie. It was his intention to seize her and, by force, celebrate his marriage to her then and there. The minute his troops and banners were sighted, Philippe de Montauban knew what was about to happen.

"You will be captured, Your Grace!" he cried. "We have not enough men to oppose them!"

"It is not a committee of welcome, then," Anne said wistfully. "I hardly expected it would be, and I recognize the banner of Alain d'Albret. What do you advise?"

"We have no choice, Your Grace. We must retreat."

"No choice," repeated Anne. "Yes, we must retreat this time. But I will make a choice of a husband and stop this madman—and very soon!"

At the command of their officers, the little company turned and galloped hard for Redon, pennants flying, colors blazing against the black sky.

Anne had not yet been crowned Duchess of Brittany, and her people had been clamoring for the ceremony to take place. Since it could not be in the capital city of Nantes, it must be in a city loyal to the young sovereign. When Anne and her party reached Redon, they were met by a delegation from the city of Rennes, which was not far distant, begging that she and her small army honor them by proceeding immediately to their city where the coronation might take place according to the ancient custom. Moreover, pleaded the dignitaries, in Rennes she would be safe from her enemies. They did not like to have her wandering about the country with so small a force. Anne was moved to tears by the speeches of her faithful subjects and decided to accept their invitation.

When she arrived at the city, she was taken to a dwelling on the river outside the city walls in the enclosure of the old abbey of Saint-Melaine. There she was dressed in an elaborate costume befitting a duchess. That evening a procession arrived, led by dignitaries of the city. They conducted her to the moat opposite the main gate of the city, the Porte Mordelaise. There they left her standing alone while they crossed the bridge and the drawbridge was raised. Alone, on the edge of the moat, the scene lighted by a thousand torches, Anne raised her young voice, which trembled a little, and pronounced the oath to maintain the privileges, liberties, and immunities of the Church, of the nobles, and of the people of Brittany. The crowd shouted their welcome, and chains rattled as the drawbridge was lowered. The two portals of the gate opened, and *Madame la Duchesse de Bretagne* was invited to enter her new capital. Around her the trumpets called a gay salute as she walked with firm steps along the square and up the ascent to the cathedral. She knew what was expected of her. It had been the custom for centuries for each new ruler to pass the night alone in the cathedral, in prayer. Guarded from a distance by her courtiers, Anne remained alone before the lighted altar, praying for strength and wisdom and for her country's future.

Day came and she was conducted to the palace. Soon the streets were filled with people, and the clergy advanced to meet her, clad in their silks of gold and purple. On the way back to the cathedral, Anne walked behind the Bishop of Rennes. At her side walked two prelates, and just behind her came the faithful Philippe de Montauban. After him marched all the courtiers of Brittany and then the nobles. Yet they were not all there. The Marshal de Rieux was missing, as was Alain d'Albret, and so, too, was Madame de Dinan—traitors all.

Under the vaulted arches of the cathedral, Anne, the crown on her head, listened to the voice of the Bishop.

"Do you swear by God and Saint Peter, into whose keeping was placed the Holy Church, and by the Evangelists whose holy relics are here present, that the liberties, freedoms, and immunities and ancient customs of the Church of Rennes, of us and our people, will be protected by you and not in-fringed?"

"Amen," answered the young voice, clear and strong. By this one word, before all the people, Anne was the crowned Duchess of Brittany, sovereign lady of the earth and the sea, mistress of the soil and the people on it in the entire nine bishoprics, ruler of all Bretons. Those who did not know her looked at her small yet resolute figure and murmured to one another. "Can a child fulfill all the duties of a sovereign?" But Montauban smiled. He was not worried; she had already been the ruler for five months.

Those five months had not been happy ones. Not only was the civil war a constant threat to security, but she had learned that some people would do dreadful things for money. Through his spies, Montauban had acquired a list of all the Breton nobles who had been in the pay of France, some of them for years. Their names were set down, together with the yearly bribe they had received. Anne was not surprised at some of the names, but others made her grieve: Madame de Dinan, the Marshal de Rieux, Jean de Rohan! There were even several churchmen. One name made her cry out in dismay—François d'Avaugour, her half brother and knight-at-arms was receiving an annual pension! Many had become voluntary exiles, but as for the others—she hardened her heart and signed a document decreeing that the traitors should be punished.

Anne had a strong feeling that she was the protector of her people, and she wanted them all to see and know her—not only those in the cities, but those in the villages and hamlets throughout her country. She announced in March, 1490, that she wished to make a journey throughout Brittany to get acquainted with her people. With the southern part of her country in French hands and war parties roving the land, this seemed the height of folly. Her council demurred, but she insisted.

"Do not leave us—your subjects!" cried the people of Rennes.

"But the people in the villages and the other cities are my subjects, too," she answered them. Finally she had her way, and the greatest precautions were taken to insure her safety. It was a rough trip with bad weather—rainy and windy—but Anne did not complain. She changed her fine clothes for simple garb more suitable to the weather and the countryside.

Two and a half years of war had left the land without good roads, and March was a bad time of year in any case; but the young Duchess managed to reach many out-of-the-way places where her presence restored order. She meted out justice where it was needed, and the peasants were touched and delighted that she had come at a sacrifice of comfort to make herself known to them. "Our good Duchess," they called her everywhere, so "Anne, the good Duchess," she became to history. With her small guard, she returned to Rennes after several weeks, feeling even more thoughtful than when she had set out. Her task was great, but she meant to accomplish it.

When she dismounted from her coach at the Porte Mordelaise, the waiting crowd was astonished to see that she was wearing wooden shoes—*sabots!* They were the only practical thing for the country she had been through, but never before had the people seen a royal person in wooden shoes. She was further endeared to her people by thus seeming to be one of them and she was called thereafter *"La Duchesse aux Sabots de Bois."* There is a legend that a man brushed through the crowd as she stepped out of the coach, knelt before her, offered her a sprig of vervain, and made this speech: "The vervain is the sacred plant of our great branch of the Celts of Gaul. We offer this symbol of our country and our race. At the moment this sprig has no leaves and no buds. But guard it well, O Duchess, for its omen is certain to come true. If it flourishes, you will be Queen." From this legend a folk song arose which is sung to this day. It is called *Avec Mes Sabots— With My Wooden Shoes.*

S'il fleurit je serai reine
Avec mes sabots—don daine
Oh, oh, oh—
Avec mes sabots.

Anne was their Duchess, of course—but Queen?

Anne's government was in difficulties. English soldiers had come to her aid, as promised by Henry VII, but they had to be paid, as did the German mercenaries who had been engaged, and her treasury was becoming depleted. A proclamation had gone out from Nantes that the government of Rieux and Albret was the true government of Brittany, so she could not expect revenue from Nantes nor from the cities in the hands of the French. It was now even more necessary to settle the matter of her marriage quickly.

Little choice was left her, but Anne determined to do her best for Brittany. She sent messengers to the court of Maximilian of Austria, accepting his offer of marriage and imploring that he give the matter his immediate attention. She was not happy about this decision, but he was the least objectionable candidate. What did it matter that she ignored the Treaty of Verger and did not consult the King of France? Of whom would he approve as her husband other than a French baron or vassal? Brittany was fighting for her life against France. Perhaps Maximilian would prove a valuable ally. Anne knew that she was not desired by this powerful ruler because of her grace, intelligence, or courage, but only for her inheritance. That he offered her a royal crown—in fact, an imperial crown —was flattering. But she was influenced most of all by the fact that his kingdom was far from her duchy, and it would not be possible for him to annex her lands to his, as would be the case with France.

Maximilian would be Duke of Brittany, and she would be Duchess of Brittany. But she would also be Duchess of Austria and Queen of the Romans! That was an exciting prospect, even though she would have to leave her beloved country for a foreign land.

The negotiations for this marriage took many months. Maximilian sent a deputation to Rennes, composed of the Count de Nassau, Wolfgang de Polhaim, who was Marshal of the Empire, and a secretary, a mayor, and a large escort. The first benefit to be realized from this proposed alliance was the capitulation of the rebel leaders at Nantes. Rieux, Madame de Dinan, and Albret asked permission to come to Rennes, hoping, of course, to gain more by submission than by holding out. The Duchess Anne called together the Estates General of Brittany to consider the terms of the alliance with Austria, as was customary in a marriage of state.

After much deliberation, a contract was drawn up and accepted by the Austrian delegation. There were ten points safeguarding the independence of Brittany, the young Duchess, and the succession. If the Austrian duke died without an heir, Anne was to be free to return to Brittany. If she should die first, childless, he would not lay claim to her duchy; he would levy no taxes nor appoint governors without the consent of the barons, nor force Brittany to go to war against her will. The first son of the marriage must be brought up in Brittany, and if there were several children, the eldest might inherit Austria, but the second should be Duke or Duchess of Brittany.

Upon formal acceptance of the terms, the next event in order was a marriage by proxy. Wolfgang de Polhaim would represent Maximilian. On the nineteenth of December, 1490, the Bishop of Rennes celebrated a pontifical Mass in the cathedral. It was attended by all the nobles and dignitaries and as many of the common people as could squeeze in or crowd the square outside. The Austrian representative placed in the hands of a canon of the church a handsome gift of gold to be used for his order. After that, a banquet was served in the chateau. When evening came, the Germanic part of the proxy marriage took place and, because it was unknown in the west, it struck the spectators as slightly ridiculous. In the presence of the whole Breton court and as many of the foreign representatives as could be accommodated in her chamber, Anne was made to lie in her bed, and Polhaim, having bared his right leg to the knee, sat on the bed and placed his leg beneath the covers. He remained there a moment, then withdrew his leg and put on his stocking. By this act, Anne was declared the wife of Maximilian of Austria. The Bretons politely concealed their smiles, and Anne, who was exhausted by the day's events, rose from her bed and received the congratulations of her new subjects and the warm good wishes of her old friends. For two weeks there was feasting and reveling by all—at great expense to the city of Rennes. From that time on, all official acts in Brittany were made "in the name of Maximilian and Anne, King and Queen of the Romans, Duke and Duchess of Brittany."

Anne seemed to have outwitted her other suitors and to have brought the rebels back to her court. The marriage, of course, was not in accordance with the stipulations of the

Treaty of Verger, and Anne had not even informed Charles VIII that it was taking place. He knew about it, however, for French spies were everywhere. Moreover, Alain d'Albret could not, after all, sustain the blow to his pride that Anne's refusal of him had inflicted, and the day following the marriage, he and his followers galloped to Nantes, which was still controlled by the rebel company of Gascon soldiers. He sent word to the King of France that the way was open and that Nantes was his if he would meet certain terms. Charles lost no time in replying to the invitation. In January, 1491, he, Anne de Beaujeu, and a great number of retainers established the court of France at Nantes. And Albret, a traitor to Brittany, having renounced all claims to the duchy, received from the French a generous yearly pension for life. Anne had, for the time being, saved herself, but she had not saved Brittany from the French, who were now more firmly than ever entrenched upon her soil.

CHAPTER V

Disaster Turned to Triumph

THE POSITION of Anne as Duchess of Brittany was desperate. With the court of the French king established in her own city of Nantes and with a number of other Breton cities in his hands, she forgave Rieux for deserting her and urged him to take some military action against her enemy. Accordingly, he set forth with a small army. Anne went part of the way, dressed in green velvet and riding a beautiful bay horse, hoping by her presence to encourage the Breton soldiers who were so few against so many. Her action did, indeed, result in the recapture of several towns from the French. Heartened by these victories, Rieux laid siege to Brest, but although the siege lasted three months, his funds for supplying food and pay to his soldiers ran out, and he was obliged to return to Rennes without recovering the city.

When, a few months earlier, Anne had returned from her expedition with the army, her fears for her country were temporarily overcome by a more personal matter. Her dearly loved sister was very ill. Twelve-year-old Isabeau had never had a firm hold on life, and now a sudden illness swept her away in only a few days. Anne was deeply grieved, and her only comfort was that she had come back in time to be with her little sister when she died. The young Duchess bore her sorrow and loneliness bravely as she turned her thoughts back to affairs of state.

The Marshal de Rieux disliked to bring up the question of money before a council presided over by a young girl who had never had to consider how much anything cost. But he knew she had been informed of Brittany's financial state soon after her father's death, and in this emergency he had no choice.

"Our funds are exhausted," he said. "Without money we cannot fight. How are we to pay the mercenaries we must have if we are to withstand the French?"

"I will give you my jewels," announced Anne. "You should be able to get a great sum for them from the moneylenders. They are of gold and precious stones—and they are very beautiful!" Her eyes filled with tears. Many rings were heirlooms— some had belonged to her mother—and all had been given her by her father. It was hard for her to think of giving them up, for they represented Brittany's former splendor. But she did not begrudge donating them to the cause of freedom.

"Oh, Your Grace, if only it were not necessary . . ."

She did not hesitate. "Sell them," she ordered.

"This loan—and it is only a loan, Your Grace—will save us for a time, and maybe our fortune will improve!" Rieux shook his head. He had been a rebel, but now he was doing his best for Brittany.

During the last months, Anne had sent urgent letters for more troops to Henry VII of England and to Maximilian of Austria. The latter, of all people, should send large forces to protect her, if not for her own sake, then for the sake of his claim, as her husband, to the Duchy of Brittany. Sitting in a little oratory in the castle at Rennes where she spent much of her time in prayer, Anne waited, week after week, for the reinforcements to come. When they eventually arrived, they were insufficient as well as too late. Some English troops landed in May, and some Spanish soldiers, dispatched by Maximilian to aid her, came soon after. But by this time, Charles VIII had amassed a very large army under the command of General La Tremouille. By the end of July, they arrived beneath the walls of Rennes, and the forces were spread out to surround it entirely, cutting off the Duchess and her court, her fourteen thousand soldiers, and all the townspeople from contact with the outside world. Thus began the siege of Rennes.

In the fourteenth and fifteenth centuries, the siege had become the most effective form of warfare. Part of the reason for this lay in the type of armor worn by the knights in the latter years of the Middle Ages. Chain mail had given way to armor plate, which, although it offered greater protection from arrows and spears, was so heavy that the horses, wearing armor plate themselves and especially bred for strength and endurance, could scarcely move under the burden of a fully armed knight. Moreover, a knight thrown from his horse was completely helpless, and without the aid of his squire, could not even get up on his feet. He could only lie on his back like an overturned beetle and this, of course, put him at the mercy of his enemy, who could easily give him a sword thrust through the joints of the iron plates. It is a wonder that *any* battles were fought on horseback, but, of course, both sides had the same handicap. By the fourteenth century, archers, crossbowmen, and pikemen had become the most important part of an army. These, pouring out a deadly rain of arrows, preceded the horsemen in an attack and the latter had only short distances to ride. Sieges, however, were an easier way of waging war. A castle had defenses and with arrows, large stones, boiling oil, and, finally, with battle-axes, could wreak havoc on men attempting to scale its walls. But storming a castle was not tried until the besieged had been weakened by starvation. Charles VIII, encamped with his large army around the walls of Rennes, could afford to wait. However, for the purpose of forcing a surrender, La Tremouille had brought with him engines of war—catapults and scaling towers—all so heavy and cumbersome that it required three thousand horses to draw them into range.

Inside the castle, Anne waited, too, and prayed and wept. She missed her beloved little sister, who had been her confidant. There was no one now to whom she could open her heart. Her governess had betrayed her once; and though she had been granted forgiveness, Anne could not again wholly trust her. During the first weeks of the siege, she waited with hope for more help from Maximilian. He could have sent an army large enough to attack the French from the rear and thereby raise the siege. But no army came.

Maximilian was not heartless; he was faced with a dilemma. His young daughter was betrothed to Charles VIII, and he therefore wanted peace with France. On the other hand, he was legally married to Anne, and he did not want to see Brittany, which he possessed jointly with her, fall to the French. He was engaged in a furious war of words. Both he and Charles were continually sending messages to all foreign princes whose lands bordered theirs, as well as to general assemblies of those countries, each of the two monarchs trying to substantiate his claim to Brittany. "When I took the Duchess of Brittany in marriage," Maximilian wrote to the Diet of Nuremburg, "and the French heard of it, they seized the city of Nantes by treachery, which gives me great regret, for I should rather have lost my own fatherland than to have suffered the outrage the French have perpetrated." However, his protests were limited to words. He could have raised additional troops, but it was a long, long way from Austria to Brittany.

The siege of Rennes had gone on for three months, and hope had not yet turned to despair within the walls when an event occurred which could only have happened in the Age of Chivalry. It was November first, All Saints' Day, and in the brightly colored tents surrounding the city there was great boredom. Life was easy for the besiegers and food was plentiful. Though the Breton knights and the mercenaries were not well fed, they were still looking for rescue and were in a mood for entertainment. When a lookout from one of the towers ran to the Marshal de Rieux with the news that a French knight in full armor was riding toward the castle, the parapets were immediately crowded with Breton men-at-arms eager to know what this might mean, for the horseman was too brilliantly attired to be a messenger.

The rider hailed the castle. "I am the Chevalier de Foix,"

he called. "Is there anyone who will break a lance with me in honor of the ladies?" Awaiting his answer, he put his horse into a canter and rode in a circle where all could see. He was dressed in red and gold, with a long scarlet cape swinging over his gleaming mail and his red plume flying in the breeze, and with one gauntleted hand he held a pennant-tipped lance upright in its socket.

A hurried conference on the castle walls produced so many volunteers that the Marshal was obliged to make the choice, and soon a Breton knight presented himself outside the castle walls to accept the challenge. This was not a battle but a game, and so it must have spectators. The lists, lined with fluttering pennants, were set up in the city square, and the stands were soon crowded by knights and ladies, as well as townspeople. In spite of the fact that she could not consider this a gala occasion, the young Duchess presided, sitting in a box provided for her halfway down the tourney field. By permission of the governor of the castle, an equal number of French knights and their ladies were admitted to the city for the tournament. The presence of the French ladies was not surprising, for it was the custom, during a siege, for officers' wives to join them in camp. The challenger and his opponent appeared and made obeisance to the Duchess and her court. They then rode to opposite ends of the lists and faced each other. A row of trumpeters raised their slender horns, and as the call to combat sounded, the two knights rode toward each other with lowered lances and clashed in mid-field. Their lances shattered, but neither knight was thrown. Five times they rode at each other, and five lances were broken by each contestant amid roars and cheers from the crowd. The knights then dismounted and unsheathed their swords. They fought long and hard, but by evening, though both were tired out, neither was injured, for they were perfectly matched in the skill of jousting. The combat was declared a draw, a judgment that satisfied everyone, whereupon refreshments of hippocras —a cordial made of spiced wine—and pastries were served to the French as well as Breton spectators.

At the end of the day, the French party withdrew to their tents. Everyone had had a good time, but the war was on again. In fact, the very next day a sortie from the castle was made by some of the mercenaries—a sortie that resulted in great carnage, and many in their group were taken prisoner by the French.

From that time on, conditions in the besieged city worsened and soon became unbearable. Anne found herself surrounded not only by the French but, within the city, by the now almost unmanageable mercenary soldiers. They had been hired to fight, and they were used to fighting for the sake of the loot they would acquire from the vanquished, taking their chances on being killed in battle. But a siege was a different thing entirely. Deprived of the opportunity to loot an enemy, they turned to stealing and destroying within the city they had been hired to defend. Since they outnumbered the Breton soldiers, it was impossible to keep them within bounds. Besides their greed for spoils, there was the matter of their pay. Anne's treasury was now empty. She had already ordered sold or mortgaged all her jewels and also her golden dishes and ornaments. Even the priceless vessels that had held holy water in the cathedral had been sold. Yet she had not enough to pay the mercenaries who were turning into vultures. She had al-

ready been forced to issue a sort of monetary substitute called
"black money"—pieces of black leather with a dot of silver in
the middle—but now these were being refused. Shops were
looted and wine merchants slain so that the soldiers could
drink their fill without paying. What they could not drink,
they sold. When townspeople, under the cover of night, made
a foray to get food, they were often stopped by the soldiers,
and the food for which they had risked their lives was seized
without payment. A siege without and anarchy within!

The month of November passed as one continuous riot and,
though guarded, the Duchess hardly felt safe in her own castle.
Affairs were in such a state that some of the English officers,
unable to restrain their men, asked permission to make their
way out of the city to the seacoast where their ships were waiting. Anne was obliged to refuse, for without them, a third of
her force at least, she had no chance at all. Supported though
she was by the council, it was Anne who made the decisions—
little Anne, only fifteen years old! She knew by now that
Maximilian, with whom only desperation had caused her to
make an alliance, was not going to help her further. With her
treasury empty, her people starving, and enemies both without
and within the city of Rennes, she knew the time had come to
sue for peace. It was not an easy thing to do, but it was agreed
among her advisers that she had no other choice.

For his part, Charles was becoming anxious. Rennes had
held out a long time. While his men were foraging for food
in the nearby towns and fields, he knew that those within the
city must be getting hungrier and hungrier. He was not a
hardhearted youth, and this worried him. Most of all, he wondered about the little Duchess, of whom he had heard so much

but whom he had never seen. How was he to approach her for a settlement? Brittany must be his—on this he was determined. That this should come to pass had been his father's goal, and now it was his. But he wished to go about it in an amiable way. His chief counselors spoke to him of his cousin, Louis d'Orleans, who had seen Anne several times and knew her father well. Perhaps Louis was the one to persuade her to give in and accept defeat. But Louis was not available. He had been imprisoned for three years because of his part in the rebellion of the princes against the regency of Anne de Beaujeu. He was now at the Château de Bourges. Could he be released and act as their envoy to Anne?

Charles thought that he could, and without informing his still vengeful sister, he immediately sent several of his trusted officers to liberate Louis and bring him to the camp before Rennes.

Louis was overjoyed at his release. Though a privileged prisoner, lodged in comfortable apartments and wanting for nothing, his inactivity had chafed him. He detested being confined and without influence at this critical time. Charles, informed of his near arrival, rode out a few miles to meet him. They embraced—Charles with genuine enthusiasm for this cousin whom he had admired when he was a child and had for years forgotten; Louis with tolerant affection for this young king, eight years his junior, who might have interfered on his behalf any time in the last three years.

"Ah, my dear cousin, I am so glad to see you!" cried the King. "And I want you to know that your imprisonment was none of my doing."

Louis smiled at the twenty-one-year-old monarch. "That I know well," he replied. "How is your dear sister?"

"She has not mellowed with the years," Charles answered ruefully. "But I am king now, and I intend to manage affairs of state myself."

"Believe me, cousin, I am greatly in your debt for having rescued me from oblivion."

"As you may guess," said Charles, "I have a reason. I want you to be my ambassador to that stubborn girl within those gray stone walls."

Louis had been kept informed of all that had happened during his imprisonment, and he knew in how hopeless a position the Duchess Anne found herself now. He had been fond of her father, and he remembered her to be a charming child. He knew that she had no other course but to surrender, and he hoped that Charles would be generous.

"I will do my best for you, Charles—Your Majesty," he said lightly. "What do you want me to do?"

The King's council met that evening, and the next day Louis d'Orleans, accompanied by the Duke de Bourbon, rode to the gate of the city and had a herald announce that they had come to parley. When they were admitted, they were appalled by the signs of famine that they saw on every side and by the noise of rioting in the streets. They were conducted to a room of state where Anne and her advisers received them in silence. Louis and his companion bowed low to the Duchess, and Anne inclined her head gravely. Louis saw that she had matured in face and figure since he last saw her, but though she held her head proudly in this hour of defeat, there was still the same sweetness about her that he remembered.

"I bring good tidings, Your Grace," he said formally. "King Charles has a proposal to make that will end this struggle and this needless suffering. Believe me, I have only your best interests at heart when I beg you to agree to his offer." With that, he proffered a parchment listing the proposed terms of peace between France and Brittany. Without reading it, Anne handed it to her Chancellor.

"Thank you, cousin. You shall have your answer as soon as we have given this due consideration. If you and the Duke de Bourbon will withdraw, refreshment will be served to you in the antechamber."

The two noblemen bowed low again and left the council to its debate. The terms offered by France were severe. Anne must give up all claim to Brittany, which Charles considered already his by right of conquest; she should marry a French prince—Louis de Luxembourg, the Duke de Nemours, or the Count d'Angoulême; she might live wherever she pleased, except at Nantes or Rennes; France would give her an allowance of 3000 *écus* a year.

The Breton council deliberated upon these terms for some hours, but from the first, Anne was firm in her refusal. She finally summoned Louis and gave him her message to the King. "Tell him," she said "that we refuse his terms. I could not in any case marry a French prince, for I am already married, as he well knows. And if, by any chance, I should become a widow, I would marry only a king or a king's son, for I am now a queen and will go no lower."

"Your Grace," said Louis, "your people are starving. You must be reasonable."

"You have my answer, Monseigneur," Anne said haughtily. "I know our desperate condition, but I will not give up my country to a man who has wrought havoc on our land for three whole years!"

Louis saw the imperious set of her mouth and shook his head sadly. "I fear you will have to submit eventually, *Madame la Duchesse!*"

Charles' next move was to send his spies to penetrate the ranks of the mercenaries. He offered to give them their overdue pay and, in addition, a bonus, if they would desert the Duchess and go home. Many of them accepted this offer, for, having been hired for money, they had no loyalty to a government that could not pay them.

This left the Breton government worse off than before. If they had little bargaining power when the first terms were offered, now they had even less. The people of the south had accommodated themselves to their French masters, but those of the north and west were still fiercely determined to be independent. Anne agreed with these subjects, who sent countless messengers to her at Rennes, but being more aware than they of the pitiful state of her military and financial ability to stand firm, she was in despair. What could a young girl with no money and only a handful of followers do against this powerful enemy?

Negotiations continued. A second offer was made to defeated Brittany so that the province might have peace with dignity, though to many it seemed like peace without honor. Charles offered to evacuate his troops immediately, pay off the remaining German, English, and Spanish mercenaries, and give the Duchess of Brittany a substantial sum each year as *rent* for the duchy. This would set her free to join her husband in Austria. But she must leave her claim to possession of Brittany to a committee of arbitration who would settle the rights of succession between herself and Charles.

To these terms, Anne was at last obliged to agree. She considered the advantages. The hated French would be gone, the soldiers would be paid and the rioting stopped, and her people in Rennes would no longer starve.

As for herself—could she expect any arbitration to save her position as Duchess of Brittany when she could not protect her title by force of arms? How would Maximilian look upon her when she fled to him—a wife without a dowry! That humiliation she could not bear to think about!

Charles carried out his part of the bargain. In a matter of weeks, there were no more French troops in Brittany except in the seaports and in his court at Nantes. The cities were at peace, trade began again, and wagonloads of produce poured into Rennes. There was nothing to prevent Anne from packing up her belongings and setting forth to join her husband, Maximilian, King of the Romans. Yet she did not go. Delay after delay occurred to put off the final parting for faraway Austria and its ruler. She had never seen Maximilian. She had no idea what life would be like in this foreign land. And who, she kept asking herself, would be the protector of her homeland when she, its rightful sovereign, was in exile? Thinking of these things, she became worried and fretful and could not bring herself to order her ladies to start packing.

It was now that the people of Brittany made their voices heard. In the cities, the villages, the countryside—even in the palace—there were murmurings, protests, then outright demonstrations, which neither the Duchess nor the French had

counted on. The cause was very simple. Her subjects did not
want Anne to go away. They loved her, first of all because she
was *"la Duchesse"*—no treaty could change that for the people
—but also because she was helpless and unhappy. And if she
went away, would she ever come back? They were afraid that
would be impossible. Therefore, if Brittany belonged to
France by right of conquest—so the talk ran—would it not be
better to accept the King of France with good grace? He was
young, generous, and powerful—not like his hated father,
Louis XI. If their beloved Duchess should marry, not a French
prince, but the King himself, she could stay at home and be
not only their duchess but their queen! This was the solution
to Brittany's problems that was on every tongue, and it was
particularly popular with the members of Anne's court, for
they realized that in this direction their own best interests lay.

Possibly Anne herself saw this as the best way out of her
difficulties. Charles had not actually proposed himself as a
suitor, but there had been hints of it in her talks with Louis
d'Orleans. She had been taught to hate French rulers as her
worst enemies, but when she considered the matter, she realized that it was Louis XI and Anne de Beaujeu whom her
father had hated. Charles had mitigated the terms of the
Treaty of Verger for her father, and though the deeds of the
last three years had been done in his name, she knew that
until very recently his sister had actually ruled. Anne did not
know him, but neither did she know Maximilian!

However, if in her inmost thoughts she ever considered
marriage with Charles, she did not speak of it but instead
offered strong objections to such an alliance. She was already
married! Being very pious, she felt that a marriage consecrated

by the church—even a marriage by proxy—was binding until
dissolved by the head of the church. Charles, too, was bound
by a contract solemnized several years before, which required
that he marry Marguerite, Maximilian's daughter, who was
living at the French court and, though a child, was being
treated as the future queen. Surely a marriage based on a
double perjury could not turn out well! Yet Anne's counsel-
lors, and even the Bishop of Rennes, urged her that this was
the best course. They were sure that, taking into consideration the circumstances, the Pope would approve and absolve
both the young people of their earlier vows.

On the French side, King Charles was being counseled in
the same direction. It was not a new thought to him. He had
heard Anne described by his cousin Louis, who admired her
sincerely. She was young, beautiful, and, actually, at his mercy.
This appealed to his chivalric nature. She needed his protection. Had she not sent him word that if free of her marriage
by proxy she would marry no less than a king? While delibera-
tions were going on and Anne's departure for Austria continued to be delayed, Charles made up his mind. His long-
winded advisers might talk on endlessly, but he would act!
Dispensing with the entourage that generally followed him,
he picked an escort of fifty archers and, attended by only a
few squires, set out for an announced pilgrimage to the
Church of Notre Dame on the outskirts of Rennes. He did,
indeed, stop there for devotions; but having finished, he and
his escort departed at a gallop for the city. When he arrived
there, the astonished soldiers, recognizing him, opened the
gates. He continued on, horses' hoofs clattering on the cob-
bles, up the hill to the chateau.

Anne was looking out an upper casement, idly watching the approaching horsemen. A few minutes later, she was amazed to hear her usher announce in the great hall below: "His Majesty, Charles the Eighth of France!"

With great dignity, though with a fast-beating heart, she drew her white robes about her—she was still wearing white in mourning for Isabeau—and descended the long stone stair-case to meet the young king who had taken from her every-thing but her pride. She had summoned her lords and ladies; and, though she was still mistress of the castle, she came down to him since he was above her in rank and also could, by right, consider himself a conqueror. But when the formalities had been dispensed with, Charles surprised everyone by bowing low before her and requesting, in a most humble tone, that he might have the privilege of a private interview. Anne was regarding with curiosity this young man whom she had always considered her enemy, and when, almost in a daze, she in-clined her head in assent, he dismissed his guard and she, in turn, dismissed her courtiers. Charles politely held out his hand, she rested hers lightly upon his wrist, and he led her to a bench by an open casement, where she seated herself. He stood before her and began to talk—at first, mere pleasantries and inquiries about her health and then, as he gazed at her sweet face and slender figure, more ardently about the matter that concerned them both.

Charles was small in stature and could not be considered by any standards a handsome man. He had a large, aristocratic nose, which was out of all proportion to his other features, but he had a firm mouth and beautiful, expressive brown eyes. When he looked at Anne, gracious and charming to a degree he had not anticipated, he was moved to show, both in his eyes and in his words, the admiration he felt for her. In a day when those of royal blood so seldom had a chance to marry for love, he felt that Divine Providence had brought them together.

To her surprise, Anne saw that he came to her, not as a conqueror, but as a lover beseeching her to take pity on him. She thought of her other suitors—the horrible Albret, the Count de Rohan's little sons, and Maximilian of Austria, a husband whom she had never seen and who had not cared enough to send sufficient help for her defense! Then she looked again at the King of France. If he was not tall, why, neither was she; if he had an enormous nose, she, too, had a defect—a limp. But he was handsomely dressed, courteous, and generous; he was the ruler of the most powerful kingdom in Europe; and he was young! She was nearly sixteen and he was only twenty-one. Would it not be wise to give in to the entreaties of her council and her people and, after begging the Pope to annul her foolish marriage with Maximilian, to ally herself with this young king who seemed suddenly to desire her? He did not want her for her lands—those he possessed already. And when a contract was made between them, perhaps she might influence him to save some independence for her beloved Brittany.

Their interview lasted more than an hour, and when it was over, there was no longer any question of their being enemies. Each had had a glimpse of personal happiness as the most unexpected end to all their difficulties, and their faces were suffused with joy. When the courtiers were called back into the great hall, the Duchess Anne had an announcement to make. *"Messieurs et Mesdames,"* she said, "you will be pleased to hear that His Majesty, the King of France, and I have resolved our differences. We have decided to marry—and as soon as possible!"

The courtiers, astonished that what they wanted had happened so suddenly, murmured their approval, then started clapping and chattering excitedly. They pressed about the royal couple who stood, hand in hand, looking at each other shyly. The lackeys spread the news to the soldiers, and a great cheer went up that seemed to shake the old castle to its foundations.

CHARLES VIII

CHAPTER VI

Queen of France

IT WAS A RADIANT ANNE who entered the chapel of the Château de Rennes three days later for the betrothal ceremony. The worries of the last three years and the enmity toward France that she had known all her life had vanished completely. Though it was late November, it seemed like June. The sun and the fresh air had taken on magical qualities. No more war, no more starving people, no more fear! She was to be married to the King of France!

Only the most privileged were invited to attend them when the two sovereigns plighted their troth—Louis d'Orleans, the Prince d'Orange, the Count de Dunois, Philippe de Montauban, and Anne de Beaujeu. A treaty of peace between France and Brittany was signed, and the marriage ceremony was set for the earliest date possible. It must take place in France, and Charles, considering his chateaux, their condition and their distance from Rennes, decided upon the Château de Langeais, one of several built during his father's reign.

Everyone in Brittany and in France seemed overjoyed at
the solution to the long years of war and intrigue. Everyone
was happy except Wolfgang de Polhaim, the ambassador from
Maximilian of Austria, who had officiated at the marriage by
proxy. Unaware of the betrothal, which Anne and Charles
had taken great pains to conceal from him, he was stunned
when a page delivered to him a large parchment on which he
read that he was invited to be present on Wednesday, December 6, at the Château de Langeais, for the wedding of Charles
VIII, King of France, and Anne, Duchess of Brittany! On behalf of his master, he was understandably indignant. He expressed his outrage to anyone who would listen, but none of
the courtiers seemed particularly interested. Still shouting his
vengeance, he took his fastest horse and departed immediately
for the north to inform the King of the Romans of this treachery on the part of the Duchess of Brittany.

As for Anne, she had been so thoroughly assured by her
ministers and churchmen, including the Bishop of Rennes,
that the proxy marriage would be annulled that she looked
forward to a real marriage with a free heart. Mounted on his
best warhorse, Charles left for the valley of the Loire on the
evening of the betrothal. Anne followed a few days after,
escorted by Philippe de Montauban and accompanied by her
ladies-in-waiting and her knights-at-arms. This was the most
important occasion of her life, and she intended to make the
most of it. Her ladies had spent the few days and nights before
her departure feverishly preparing her wardrobe. Anne's taste
had always been for the elegant and beautiful, both in dress
and in furnishings. For several years she had been obliged to
practice the strictest economy, but now that she was to be

Queen of France, and because of the generosity of her hus-
band-to-be—her treasury was empty—she was able to dress as
befitted her role.

She arrived at the end of her journey to Langeais on horseback, wearing a black satin traveling costume that was covered
with a black velvet cloak richly furred with sables. To the
others in her party, which included her half sister Françoise,
she had presented rich clothing so that they might be clad as
was proper for a queen's retinue. The ladies wore beige satin
and black velvet; the men were in black or crimson. The
knights and ladies, followed by horses drawing velvet-trimmed
wagons that contained their beds and boxes, made a handsome
procession as they approached Langeais. They would all have
been very light at heart except for one sorrowful event. The
Count de Dunois, one of Anne's staunchest supporters in all
her troubles, had been seized with a heart attack as he galloped to overtake them, had fallen from his horse, and had
died as he was carried to an inn. But sad as it made her to lose
so valued a friend, Anne's heart could contain only eager
excitement as she arrived at the chateau where Charles was
waiting for her.

Even though there had been so little time, Charles had had
the castle decorated in Anne's honor, particularly the great
hall with its huge fireplaces at each end, its intricate tiled floor
in red and green, and its heavy, beamed ceiling. He had used
all the resources at his command. Several thousand yards of
cloth of gold and silk adorned the rooms and the chapel. The
draperies of Turkish velvet were seven yards long. There was
a table fifteen feet long with benches of equal length for the
Queen's dining room. Two beds, six feet long and six feet

wide, were for the Queen's six maids of honor, and there was
a similar bed for her several doctors, except that it was made
six and a half feet in length to accommodate their taller
stature. All the silver pieces were engraved with flowers and
Charles' motto and marked with an A and a K—K standing for
Karlos, a Latinate version of *Charles.* Plaques of walnut,
carved with the lily of France and the ermine of Brittany,
were hastily installed, and on them the A and K were inter-
twined. Anne, who was making her first visit outside of Brittany, was delighted with everything.

As she stood beside Charles in her wedding gown of cloth
of gold, embossed in an intricate design and trimmed with
one hundred and seventy-eight skins of sable, she smiled happily, marveling at the change that had come about in only a
few weeks. The Bishop of Albi conducted the wedding ceremony, the Bishop of Angers celebrated the Mass that followed,
and the highest ranked attendants were all, at last, her good
friends: the Duke d'Orleans, the Duke de Bourbon, Anne de
Beaujeu, the Counts de Foix, de Vendôme, and d'Angoulême,
the Prince d'Orange, the Chancellors of France and of Brittany, the Mayor of Rennes, and several merchants. It was a
brilliant assembly, and as she emerged from the great hall to
a smaller chamber to sign the marriage contract, the words of
the Bishop were still ringing in her ears. He had said: "Our
Sovereign Lord and Most Christian Prince, Charles, King of
France, the eighth of that name, at present reigning, and the
Most Noble Princess, Madame Anne of Brittany, who of their
own free will desire to be joined in Holy Matrimony . . ."

This last was very important because some nobles who were
out of favor—one of whom was the Viscount de Rohan—and

of course Maximilian had made the charge that Anne had been abducted and taken by force to Langeais. Anne had to make a statement before an ecclesiastical commission that she had gone to Langeais voluntarily and that the marriage to Charles was her own wish.

The marriage contract covered all emergencies and was most fortunately phrased for Anne's benefit. It stated that the two sovereigns were to have equal rights in Brittany and that if Anne died before her husband, the province would belong to France, but if he died first, the duchy would be returned to her to rule as before. Moreover, if Charles left Anne a childless widow and she wished to remarry, she must marry either the new king or his heir. In writing this contract, the two Chancellors had weighed every word, hoping to insure an era of peace in the war-torn land. The Bretons had not lost their Duchess. She had merely added to the crown of Noménoé the crown of France. Far from having stepped down, she had risen in power and honor, and it was as a mark of esteem that Charles arranged for her a dower, in case of his death, by which she would retain absolutely everything she possessed in France at that time. Anne was quite content. She could not see beyond her present state of bliss.

For a whole month, Charles and Anne spent a honeymoon near the Loire, principally at Tours. For that time, their responsibilities were forgotten, as were the parties and tournaments that usually marked their social life, and they were just two people in love. The dispensation from the Pope arrived a week after the wedding, so all was regularized. And because they were happy, the people were happy, too. There were many celebrations in the cities, especially in Rennes, which had quickly recovered from the siege, and many toasts were drunk to the King and his new Queen.

But affairs of state could not be put off indefinitely. Charles must take his bride to Saint-Denis, an old basilica just north of Paris, to be crowned. In January, they started out and journeyed by easy stages, stopping in each town to be greeted by joyous celebrations. They would be met outside the gates of a town or city by captains, who were always noblemen, authorized to meet and greet persons of high rank. Inside the gates or in the cathedral square, a procession was formed. It was led by the nobles, the clergy, and the municipal officers; after them came the professional men—judges, clerks, doctors, lawyers, and notaries; next came the wool merchants, small-wares dealers, and goldsmiths; and at the rear would march those of the lowest order, among whom would be the water carriers. All wore their best in honor of the occasion. In the evening, there were fireworks and dances. Since these celebrations were repeated every day, progress to Paris was very slow. On January 26, Anne had her first gay birthday in many years. She was sixteen years old, and, looking ahead, she could see nothing but happiness—tenderness from her husband and love from her people, French and Breton alike.

On February 8, 1492, as the bells rang out joyously from the tower of Saint-Denis, a happy girl mounted the platform erected in the choir of the old basilica. Her ladies, each wearing a coronet, formed a semicircle of glittering elegance in the dark church. Anne was dressed simply in a white satin gown with a train, and her dark hair fell in braids over each shoulder. The Archbishop of Bordeaux anointed her, and when he placed the huge gold and jewel-encrusted crown upon her head, the scepter in her right hand, and the hand of justice in her left, she bowed under the great weight. Because it was too large, the crown slipped over her forehead. Louis d'Orleans, standing behind her, lifted it up; and, during the long mass that followed, he continued to hold the symbol over her head, lowering it when she knelt, so that at all times she appeared dignified. This new sovereign was the child he remembered so fondly, the young duchess in whose behalf he had worked so that both Brittany and France might be at peace. Now that she was married to Charles, did he perhaps have a moment of envy?

After the coronation, the royal party took the road to Paris, a city known to Anne only by reputation but one she longed to call her own. To please the crowd, she had put on her wedding gown of cloth of gold. The streets leading to Notre Dame Cathedral were hung with banners, and members of the Parliament and officers of the City Hall formed her guard of honor. Seated on her litter, which was mounted on the backs of her favorite horses, Anne proceeded to the cathedral. There were shouts and cheers and tears and blessings from the populace. "So young! So beautiful!" they cried. "So gracious—she is like the figure of a saint!"

The city fathers had outdone themselves in her honor. The square before the cathedral was hung with tapestries, with boughs of greenery, and even with flowers, though it was winter. The Queen's litter halted in front of one of the platforms, for it was clear that costumed players waited here to perform an allegory. A man dressed as *Justice* made a speech in which he called upon all to thank God that they could here see the *lily* joined to the *ermine*. After rousing cheers, four actors representing the *Church,* the *Nobility,* the *Mer-chants,* and the *Laborers* stepped forward to clasp hands, but *War* leaped in, forcing them apart. Then, from a nearby rooftop and supported by a mechanical contrivance, *Peace* appeared as if from heaven and, descending to the ground, seized *War* by the throat and proceeded to kill him on the spot. Thereupon, two actors dressed as *France* and *Brittany* embraced each other, weeping for joy. The trumpets sounded, the crowd went wild, and Anne applauded vigorously. Her triumph was complete, and the procession moved on across the Seine to the palace of the Louvre, at that time a medieval fortress like all the other castles in France.

Anne and Charles had had more than a month of privacy in which to get acquainted with each other and to rejoice over the good fortune that had changed enmity to love. Now there were serious affairs of state that must be dealt with. First, there was the matter of twelve-year-old Marguerite of Austria, who, since the age of three, had been living in the Louvre and had been treated like the future Queen of France. Her infant betrothal to Charles had now been dissolved, but it was not to be expected that she would understand or take kindly to the older girl who had displaced her. Anne felt that her first duty was to placate this disappointed child. It was all the more necessary because this was her second humiliation of Maximilian. During her first months in Paris, Anne set about winning the respect and affection of Marguerite, and Anne could be very charming indeed. It took six months to arrange Marguerite's departure, which was accepted with good grace, if reluctantly, by that Austrian princess. During those months, Anne gave her many gifts of jewels and, as a crowning touch, she had a beautiful costume made for her by the most skillful of her maids-of-honor, to which she added some embroidery done with her own hands. On the twelfth of June, Marguerite left Paris to join her father in Flanders, and though she still felt the sting of rejection, she had a warm spot in her heart for Anne, and they corresponded as friends for many years.

While Anne could be kind and gentle with someone who had suffered misfortune, she was also haughty and proud. Trained from the cradle to be a duchess, she had been accustomed for three years to making the final decisions on the affairs of her country. These qualities came to the fore when she discovered, early in her residence in Paris, that Anne de Beaujeu, her sister-in-law and ten years her senior, expected to continue to control Charles as she had when she was regent. From force of habit, Charles had allowed his sister to exercise power, though the freeing of Louis d'Orleans and his own marriage to Anne had been acts on which he had not consulted her.

She had behaved in a very friendly manner toward the young duchess, but now that they were occupying the same residence, Charles' sister was about to receive an unpleasant surprise. This girl with the royal air was easily her match. Anne, the wife of Charles, was Queen, and she knew her prerogatives. Anne, the sister and former regent, was no longer a factor in the government.

On the surface the two women were most cordial, but the Queen knew the devious ways of her former adversary. As a precaution, in July of that first year, she had an alliance of mutual aid sworn to by Charles, Louis d'Orleans, and the Duke de Bourbon for the purpose of safeguarding the realm

and preventing intrigue by outside enemies or by friends of
Anne de Beaujeu within the kingdom. There were indeed
enemies. Many tried to prove that Brittany would be a liabil-
ity to France rather than an asset. Chief among these was the
Viscount de Rohan, whom Charles had made, before his marriage, Lieutenant General of Brittany. Now that there had
been such a radical change in the situation, Charles forced
Rohan to retire, and he was succeeded by Anne's friend and
supporter, Philippe de Montauban. Since the Prince d'Orange was already representing Anne, there were now two loyal
men working for peace and unity between France and Brittany—both Bretons—and Rohan could only grind his teeth
and wait for a chance to strike. He attempted a plot, with the
English as his allies, but it was discovered and came to nothing.

Anne actively concerned herself with these matters, but as
the year progressed, Charles made it known to her, albeit
gently, that he had been governed for years by his sister, and
he did not propose to accord his wife the same privilege. He
loved her dearly and appreciated her intellectual qualities,
but he made her understand that the business of France was
the business of the King alone and he would prefer that she
should not meddle in it. She accepted his decision gracefully
and, except for intervening in behalf of the pardon or
advancement of some individual, she never again during
Charles' reign attempted to take part in the government of
France.

It was easy for her to refrain at this time, for she was about
to become a mother, and all her thoughts were turned toward
this happy event.

CHAPTER VII

Wife and Mother

CHARLES AND ANNE considered the Château d'Amboise their home, and Charles continually added to the castle's size and furnishings. He had workmen build two magnificent stone towers, one with a stone ramp so wide that six knights abreast could ride their horses to the top. No other chateau had such a marvel. The royal couple spent some of their time, however, at another, smaller chateau—Plessis-les-Tours. Paris held no fascination for Anne, and she was glad to get away from its narrow, dirty streets, squalor, fetid smells, and raucous noises. Charles had to make many trips to the residences of his barons, for it was customary for a king to keep in close touch with his supporters. The newly wed King and Queen could not bear to be separated, so Anne went with him nearly always, traveling by boat on the rivers whenever possible—a more comfortable mode of travel for one in her condition. If her husband could not travel so slowly, she would meet him at their destination. Her ladies accompanied her, and they would amuse themselves on long journeys by playing quiet games.

So time passed, and it was with great joy that Anne looked forward to the birth of her first child. Of course it would be a son. It surely had to be when everyone wished it so ardently —a son who would grow up to be ruler over both France and Brittany! It was decided that the birth should take place at Plessis-les-Tours, and some weeks before the child was expected, cabinetmakers, tapestry weavers, and servants of all kinds went there to see that the place was well provided and properly decorated for such an auspicious event as the birth of a *dauphin*.

On October 10, 1492, the child was born, and it was the son all had hoped for. Charles immediately sent out a message to all his people:

> Friends and loyal subjects: Thanks to God and Our Lady, at about four o'clock in the morning, our very dear and much loved spouse, the Queen, gave birth to a fine son, of which fact we wished to advise you at once, knowing that it will be a great joy to you.

There was, indeed, great rejoicing throughout the entire land, for now the succession was assured.

On October 13, the infant was baptized in a most magnificent ceremony in the chapel at Amboise—an exquisite building separate from the chateau. At the chapel's rear entrance, at ten o'clock in the morning, a solemn procession formed and proceeded to the altar. It was composed of two godfathers, the Duke de Bourbon and the Duke d'Orleans; one godmother, Jeanne de Laval, Queen of Sicily—a lady very dear to Anne; the Duke de Nemours, carrying the wax candle; the

Count de Foix, carrying the golden salt cellar; the Duke de
Vendôme, carrying the ewer; the heir to the Spanish throne
with the basin and napkin; and Madame l'Admirale de Bourbon with the holy oil. The King waited in the chapel, his face
showing profound emotion, and behind him, filling the little
church and the courtyard without, stood five hundred ladies,
officers, lords, and archers. Bareheaded, wearing a long robe of
cloth of gold, the Prince d'Orange presented the newly born
child, who was then baptized and consecrated with holy oil by
a monk, François de Paul, founder of the Order of Minimes
and later declared a saint. The child was christened Charles-
Orland and, according to the wishes of his mother, was
dedicated to the Virgin.

King Charles was a romantic young man who had read all
the tales of chivalry, especially those about Charlemagne. He
and Anne had this interest in chivalry as a common bond, and
what was more natural than naming their first-born son after
a hero of the past—Roland, whose name was sometimes spelled
Orland? Charles had not had the opportunity to read widely
until after his father's death. Then, as king, he engaged tutors,
secured manuscripts, and tried to make up for the lack of
education in his early years. He would never be a scholar, but
he knew more than most young noblemen of his time. He had
a dream of conquering Italy, and once having accomplished
that, of riding like a knight errant to conquer Constantinople
and recover the Holy Land from the infidel—just as his predecessors had tried to do in the Crusades of the Middle Ages.
But he was deeply attached to Anne and to his small son, and
so he did nothing about his dreams of conquest for almost
two years.

During this time, the building and refurnishing went on,

and Amboise became filled with treasures. Anne was so gracious to the artists who came to work at the chateau that many of them stayed in her employ for years. There were goldsmiths, tapestry makers, painters, and sculptors, and it was mainly Anne who kept them busy. She had a passion for jewels—diamonds, pearls, and rubies—and she had the goldsmiths polish and set them in intricate patterns for rings, necklaces, and bracelets. The furnishings of her apartments at Nantes, her wardrobe and jewels, and her father's library—all the things that Charles had saved from plunder by Alain d'Albret—were brought to her at Amboise. She did not neglect the decoration of the beautiful little chapel, but ordered everything used there to be made of silver or gold encrusted with gems, and she had the sacerdotal vestments made of blue velvet embroidered with the lily of France. There were famous articles from the past displayed at Amboise: the sword of the legendary Lancelot; the battle-ax of King Clovis; the dagger of Charlemagne; two battle-axes used by Saint Louis; the swords of Philippe le Bel, King John, Charles VII, and Louis XI; a three-pointed ax ornamented with diamonds that had belonged to the famous Du Guesclin; and the parade armor of Joan of Arc with her gauntlets and helmet—golden armor lined with crimson satin—a treasure indeed!

Dozens of beautifully carved chests, wardrobes, and tables were made for the chateau, but few chairs, for no one sat in a chair but the King and Queen. The ladies-in-waiting either stood or sat on the floor, but if they were elderly or indisposed, low stools or cushions were provided. The gentlemen stood— such was the custom.

The care of the baby, Charles-Orland, was committed to the

best nurse that could be found, and from the first, he thrived and grew strong. It was his father's wish that he should always be dressed in white with silver trimming and wear a cloak of silver cloth. During his first months of life, Anne accompanied her husband on short journeys about the kingdom as usual and, having taken every precaution, tried not to worry about the welfare of her son. During 1492 and 1493, Charles laid plans for his expedition into Italy, where he hoped to win fame and glory, and in the spring of 1494, he could put it off no longer. He wanted to leave a glorious heritage to his son.

Italy was, at this time, a group of city states, of which the most powerful were Milan in the north, Naples in the south, and the Papal States, comprising all of central Italy. Pope Innocent VIII invited Charles to invade Naples, which was the traditional enemy of the Papal See, and promised him military help. Because Charles, fresh and eager for adventure, did not want any hindrance placed in his way, he made three treaties designed to keep other countries neutral: he restored to Spain the province of Rousillon and Cerdagne; to Maximilian he restored Artois and Franche-Comte, the two provinces which had been Marguerite's dowry; and he paid to England 745,000 *écus* of gold—all for a free hand in Italy. It was a great price to pay; Anne protested, but the King did not heed her.

"Why must you go away from me? Forget this dream of conquest!" Anne pleaded.

"But I am King. Who will remember me after my death if I stay at home in idleness?"

"You have a kingdom to govern. Is that not enough?"

"I must win fame—for the sake of our son whom we love so much."

"But the danger! I fear for your safety, Charles!"

"Do not worry, dear one. My life is in God's hands."

Anne did not remonstrate too much for, in her experience, kings and dukes were born to fight, and women could only wait and pray for their safety.

Charles wished her to accompany him as far as the Alps—to Lyons and Grenoble, where the preparations would be made for his army to start across the mountains. Very explicit commands were given for the care of their child, *Monsieur le Dauphin,* for they dared not take him on so long a journey. The chateau was to be guarded, night and day, by a detachment of one hundred soldiers—this honor being given to the Scottish Guards; hunting was forbidden in the area around the chateau; the outskirts of Amboise and even the city itself were to be carefully policed; and no stranger was to be permitted in the city except by special permission. If an epidemic occurred in any part of France, Amboise was to be immediately closed to access; and if, by an unlucky chance, disease should break out in Amboise, the Dauphin was to be transferred at once to whichever of the castles seemed safest from contagion. The young prince could be taken out for walks, even in the garden, only when accompanied by an armed force. The garrisons of nearby castles were to be ready at a moment's notice to rush to aid Amboise, and the governor of the castle and the child's nurse were to report frequently to his parents on the state of his health and affairs at the chateau. It seemed to the mother and father that they had covered every possible emergency with proper precautions, and they set out with confidence for the week's journey to the south.

The royal party made a brilliant entrance into Lyons, a city they had not before visited. Anne, preceded by six pages in crimson velvet embroidered with the letter A, was seated in a sedan chair covered with red velvet. She wore a dress of cloth of gold trimmed with ermine and fastened with diamond buttons. Her Breton cape was also of cloth of gold and was ornamented with precious stones. Her sash was gold, and her red velvet cloak, lined with ermine, fell from her shoulders to the ground. This first view of their new Queen, accompanied by the King in all his magnificence, made a deep impression on the people of Lyons.

Charles and his court spent several months in Lyons while the army was being outfitted. The troops must be provisioned for a long journey and given practice for the fighting to come. Lists were set up in different parts of the city for the jousts, tournaments, and combats, in many of which the King himself took part. Louis d'Orleans and several other nobles were the leaders, and each one wanted to have a turn with the King. Though small of stature, Charles was a very able fighter. In Lyons he had several suits of armor made, as well as the vestments he would wear over them. One was a tunic, open at the front and back, of white satin with large sleeves. It was lined with white taffeta and bordered with a band of bright gold. With this costume he was to wear a headdress with forty-eight plumes attached by gold wire.

When the preparations were completed, the royal party journeyed to Grenoble, where they were received with as much pomp as at Lyons. This was, indeed, the end of the journey for Anne. On August 29, after hearing Mass, Charles

embraced his wife and set forth at the head of his army to cross
the Alps and conquer Italy. France had no real need for more
territory, and it was pure ambition that motivated Charles.
The far-reaching result of his expedition was the bringing of
the Italian Renaissance to France.

Charles had gathered together a very large army. It contained, besides his regular soldiers, any number of cutthroats
and other kinds of criminals, as well as soldiers of fortune.
There were 3600 lances, 6000 Breton archers, 6000 crossbowmen, 8000 arquebusiers, 8000 Swiss pikemen, and a powerful
train of artillery. There was very little discipline, and Charles
counted on his personal popularity to control this vast horde,
all bent on victory and plunder.

With misgiving and sorrow, Anne watched them go. Among
the leaders were most of her friends: Louis d'Orleans, the
Dukes de Montpensier, Foix, Luxembourg, and Cleves; and
Pierre de Rohan and the Marshal de Rieux, both of whom
found adventure more appealing than plotting against their
former Duchess. She knew her husband to be brave to the
point of recklessness, and she had heard of the sinister character of the Italians. She worried about not only the sword of
the enemy but the poison of an assassin. Could any amount
of glory be worth the risks? Her only solace was prayer. To
reinforce her own petitions for Charles' safety, she made many
gifts: to the most celebrated churches of the Touraine and
Ile-de-France, she gave offerings of money for prayers for the
success of Charles' mission and safe return; to the royal Abbey
of Saint-Denis, she donated two candles weighing twenty
pounds each, one to be burned before the statue and the other
before the reliquary of the saint; and to the Convent of Notre

Dame des Anges at Lyons, she gave a bell for the tower in
return for the prayers of the nuns. Every few days, she received a letter from Charles, sent by a fast messenger; and
twice a week, she had news of her son in Amboise. From
both, the news was always good, and gradually she became
more calm.

When Charles arrived in Italy, conquest was both immediate and easy. Florence became his without violence, and his
entry into the city was magnificent. Over streets freshly
sanded by the Florentines, and between tapestries and hangings that festooned the windows, came a procession led by the
King's four drummers. After the drummers came the fifes, and
then the sergeants-at-arms, crossbowmen, archers, and the
Swiss pikemen. Then came the men-at-arms, the halberdiers,
and the heavy cavalry. The cavalrymen wore greaves on their
legs, their surcoats glittered with gold, and plumes tossed on
their leather headgear. Above them waved the pennants of
France and the ensigns of the various companies. They were
followed by the royal household—eight hundred noblemen
in gorgeous armor and more pikemen in doublets of velvet
and gold. Last of all came the King on his splendid black
charger. Charles was dressed for this occasion in golden armor
set with pearls and other precious stones, and over it a long blue
cloak fell from his shoulders and spread over the crupper of his
horse. His hat was white, encircled with a crown and topped
by a black plume, and he carried a lance. Behind him flocked
the civilians of Florence, members of the Florentine Council,
magistrates, and merchants. On this, his first official appearance in Italy, there could be no question of his welcome. A
treaty with Florence was written up and willingly signed.

But events suddenly changed the face of things in Italy. Pope Innocent VIII, who had urged Charles to come to Italy, died. And so, too, did Ferdinand of Spain, on whom Charles had counted to keep Spain neutral. The new Pope, Alexander VI, proved an enemy and urged Naples to repulse the French. He called on all of Europe to help him against the invader and even appealed to the Sultan of Turkey. Charles, undismayed, continued his march toward Rome; and because the people were friendly, the Pope now appeared to be friendly also. On December 31, Charles made a triumphal entry into Rome with his huge army and remained there for several weeks. He made an excellent impression on the citizens, for he attended Mass daily and remained kneeling with folded hands throughout the service. He allowed no excesses from his followers, and his departure was regretted when he left for Naples—his real objective in the Italian campaign.

The ruler of Naples, Alphonso II, was a cruel and vicious man, hated by his subjects. When they heard that the French army was approaching, they revolted against his orders and went out to meet their liberators. On February 22, 1495, Charles took over the city without a struggle, heard the grievances of the people, and granted them the liberties they demanded. Alphonso fled from the city.

Charles was entranced with the beauties of Naples—its art treasures, its cultivated gardens, its architecture. A letter to one of his confidants at home shows his enthusiasm:

You cannot believe what beautiful gardens I have seen in this city. Upon my faith, I think that only Adam and Eve are wanting to make them the earthly paradise, so fair are they and so full of extraordinary objects. Also I have found here the best possible painters of ceilings and there are no ceilings in Beauce, Lyons, or any other part of France which can approach in beauty those I have seen here. I will engage some of these painters and bring them with me to work at Amboise.

And this, to another of his friends:

. . . those very singular things . . . houses with sweet little windows, tall, long, wide, full galleries, pleasant gardens, little courtyards, alleys, gates, hills, rivers for enjoying yourself and frolicking, where are old statues in alabaster, white marble and also porphyry.

Charles professed that he could not bear to think of his favorite chateau, Amboise, in comparison with Italian villas! When he got home, he was going to set about changing it into the Italian style.

But much had to be done before he could return home, and he did not write to Anne about his difficulties. Things were not going well in Naples. The French soldiers got out of hand. They looted and behaved as have conquering armies of all times, and this in spite of their welcome and good treatment by the people of Naples. The trouble was that they had no fighting to do and were bored by inaction. Complaints of the soldiers' conduct were made to Charles and his barons, but they paid no attention. As their stay in Naples lengthened, word of this behavior spread to the rest of the city states, and finally all Italy became terrified of its powerful guest.

A league against France was formed by the Pope, the Dukes of Milan and Venice, and, from outside Italy, Maximilian of Austria and Isabella of Spain. Charles was furious that he had been betrayed by the two countries he had paid to be his allies, and decided to leave Naples and return home. Before leaving, he wanted to stage a triumphal entry into Naples, which he had entered informally when he arrived. Robed as an Emperor of the East, with crowned head and scepter in hand, he himself led the procession. A solemn service was held in the cathedral, and he gave a great banquet for the nobles, who came the more readily because he was about to quit their city. On May 20, leaving a lieutenant with 10,000 men to guard Naples, he started the long march back to France. Ahead of him, he sent twenty-two Italian artists—painters, architects, embroiderers, cabinetmakers, and goldsmiths. Also he was bringing with him hundreds of art objects and manuscripts—a single convoy weighed 87,000 pounds—which later decorated the chateau at Amboise.

When he arrived in Rome, he found that the Pope had fled the city and there would be no resistance. His army marched on, avoiding Florence where he had had his first welcome, and crossed the Apennines. Up to now, his had been a victorious march across Italy with an army that had not had to fight a single battle, but was now somewhat weakened by disease and debauchery. On July 6, with only 9,000 men, he met the army of Venice—40,000 men from various parts of Italy, Austria, and Spain—under the command of the Marquis of Mantua. The battle took place at Forvano on the banks of the Po River. It lasted one hour and took three thousand lives, but it was the allies of Venice who broke and fled, and the French claimed the victory. It was, however, a less jaunty army that started across the Alps with winter not far away. Meanwhile, the Neapolitans had overcome the 10,000 troops left to guard their city. Charles' expedition, which had cost a fabulous amount, had been entirely useless politically and had wasted thousands of lives, yet, in the opinion of his contemporaries, Charles had covered himself with glory.

Meanwhile, during the fifteen months that her husband was in Italy, Anne had not been able to bring herself to leave Lyons, where she was able to receive her husband's messengers without delay the moment they reached French soil. She did not even go to see her little son—a week's journey each way. The news of him was reassuring, and the desire to keep as close as possible to her husband was very strong. In August, 1495, an epidemic broke out in the town of Amboise, but she received letters, saying there was no danger—that Charles-Orland was in perfect health. The news from her husband, following the battle of Fornavo, alarmed her, and she resolved not to start north until he could join her. A few days later, however, a horseman galloped into Lyons on a lathered horse, threw himself before the Queen to present a letter, and gasped out one word: "Urgent!" Tearing open the paper she read:

Sovereign Lady and Mistress, the Queen: *Monsieur le Dauphin* is very ill. It was very sudden. Come at once if you can.

It was signed by the Governor of the Château d'Amboise. Anne, thoroughly alarmed, sent a messenger racing to the King, ordered a small force of attendants, and set out at once for Amboise. Charles, who had almost reached Lyons, left his army and galloped ahead with only a few followers. But it took days to reach Amboise, even at the fastest pace, and both parents arrived, almost together, to find that their precious child had died the day before, two months after his third birthday. They had missed a year and a half of his short life, and they were grief-stricken. "He was a handsome child," wrote a contemporary, "who spoke up boldly, not fearing the things other children usually fear."

Neither Anne of Brittany nor Charles VIII could be consoled. The people, too, were sad, for France no longer had an heir. The parents blamed themselves for leaving the child to the care of others, though the doctors had done their best, and no one could be held responsible for what was considered an act of God. They vowed that if they had another chance, they would stay close to their baby and see that no harm came to him. Charles, in particular, felt guilty that he had been off on an expedition—the glory of which seemed bitter to him now. He grieved so sincerely that his health became affected, and Anne had to set aside her own grief in an effort to drive away his melancholy. Each played a little comedy for the benefit of the other, and urged the courtiers to laugh and joke to dispel the atmosphere of sadness. When weeks had passed and there seemed no change in the King, the courtiers made up plays, staged dances, and put on pantomimes to cheer up their master and mistress. Anne found it difficult to stand the laughter and gaiety and often rebuked the lords and ladies for doing what she had originally suggested. On one occasion, Louis d'Orleans staged a masquerade in which he played the fool and danced so gaily that the Queen, whose grief made her short-tempered, berated him with such fury that he felt obliged to leave the court and retire to his chateau at Blois. A chronicler wrote:

> If she had reflected before exiling her cousin, the little Queen, so sad and hurt, would have certainly realized that

Louis d'Orleans, the most chivalrous of princes, was incapable of exhibiting before her an indecent levity, and to have profited by a masquerade to rejoice publicly in a death which brought him nearer to the throne.

It was true, indeed, that the death of the Dauphin left Louis heir apparent to the kingdom of France.

The next three years were sad and terrible. Anne and Charles wanted another child, not only to provide an heir to the throne (if it was a boy, for France was governed by the Salic Law, which forbade the kingdom to a female heir), but in the hope of finding again the joy they had experienced in the first years of the life of little Charles-Orland. On September 8, 1496, a son was born and was named Charles. The "Orland" was not added for he could not replace their first son, and perhaps the King had now changed his mind about the value of glory and adventure. Less than a month later, on October 3, the infant died. They had hardly had time to know him, and their grief was not so profound as for their firstborn. Ten months later, Anne gave birth to another son, whom they named Francis, but he lived only a few days. The bells of rejoicing at their advent had hardly stopped ringing before the deaths of these infants deprived the kingdom of an heir. And yet, Anne had scoured the country for the most learned doctors and nurses to care for her and her infants. In 1498, a daughter was born who lived only a day. Anne's despair can be imagined—in less than three years, she had given birth to three frail infants who could not survive. The people murmured that her marriage was cursed because it was based on the rejection of two solemn vows—to Maximilian and to his daughter Marguerite.

Sadly, Anne and Charles arranged with a prominent sculptor, Jean Juste, to make a splendid tomb for their lost ones. When completed, it was placed in the cathedral at Tours. There, today, atop a beautifully carved white marble base, lie the sculptured figures of the children guarded by angels— an enduring monument to love and grief.

The King was trying to recover from the grief caused by the successive deaths of his children and was undertaking the government of his kingdom with more seriousness than before. He dispensed with his advisers and tried to study and resolve all problems himself. Justice, the administration of the Church, finances, and affairs of state were all in need of reforms for which he proposed bold and generous decrees. He was also planning another, better organized expedition into Italy. He was, in fact, on the way to becoming one of France's great kings. However, Charles did not live to fulfill that promise.

On Saturday, April 7, 1498, the court was at Amboise. A tennis match was to take place that afternoon in the lowest level of the chateau, some distance beneath the ground. Anne and Charles, who planned to be present, left their apartments after the noon meal and, in order to take the shortest route, pursued their way through a narrow dark corridor that was called the "Galerie Hacquelbac." Ordinarily it would not have been used for it was full of trash. Charles did not take sufficient care, and, as he passed under a low stone archway, he struck his head with such force that he staggered. He was stunned but recovered his balance, and they continued on to the tennis court. He made a few remarks to the courtiers he found there, then broke off in the middle and collapsed.

Anne was terrified. She summoned the court physicians, but they could do nothing. They were afraid to move Charles, so they placed him on some cloaks on the stone floor of the corridor. He never regained consciousness but lay in a coma until eleven o'clock that night. Then he cried out, called on the Virgin Mary and his patron saint, stammered a hope that his sins be forgiven, and died. He was twenty-eight years old.

Except for the first two years of her marriage, Anne had had ten years filled with worry and grief. Now she was a widow at twenty-two, having lost all those dear to her—her father, her mother, her sister, four children, and, finally, her husband.

LOUIS XII

CHAPTER VIII

Brittany Again

ANNE'S GRIEF WAS PITIFUL to see. Her ladies were unable to wait on her or even to make her take notice of them. For two days she lay on the floor in a corner of her chamber, sobbing bitterly and refusing to eat. It was for such a short time that she had known complete happiness with Charles and their little son! Then had come the long time of worry while her husband was in Italy, and after that, the years of alternate hope and grief as their children were born and died. She had forced herself to be brave for Charles' sake then, but now there was no reason why she should not give way to sorrow.

Louis d'Orleans was now King of France. Affairs of state claimed his attention, but he gladly would have put everything aside to go to Anne in her desperate need, had he not been afraid that the sight of him would recall happier occasions and increase her tears. From reports he received, he was afraid that she might fall into a decline or even end her life, so in his stead he sent the Bishop of Condon—an old friend and most

venerated counsellor—to console her. It was the Bishop who
succeeded in getting her to stop crying and take something to
eat. Eloquent and understanding, acquainted with all human
suffering, he talked gently to her and comforted her, and
finally she fell into an exhausted sleep. When she awakened,
the sudden realization came to her, forgotten in her grief,
that she did have something to live for—Brittany needed her!
She had neither husband nor children, but she was once more
Duchess of Brittany. The marriage contract with Charles had
assured this. She must not fail the duchy that had been everything to her before she met Charles. Her recovery began from
that moment, and although she mourned, it was not in
despair. On the third day, she wrote to her dearest friend,
Jeanne de Laval, Queen of Sicily, telling her of the tragedy,
and soon afterward she consented to see her cousin, King
Louis XII of France.

"*Votre Majestée . . .*" the usher began, but Anne broke in,
"I no longer have that title. I am once again *Madame la
Duchesse.*"

She had a long talk with Louis and was much comforted by
his kindness. If he allowed himself to feel more than cousinly
affection for her, now that she was no longer married, he gave
no hint of it. She had agreed at Langeais that she would take
for a second husband only the King of France or his heir, but
Louis did not know whether she would consider marrying
again and this was certainly not the time to mention it. As a
matter of business, she signed a paper reestablishing the independent Duchy of Brittany and then sent word to Jean
de Chalons, Prince d'Orange, making him Premier to govern
in her absence. Then they discussed the arrangements for the

funeral and interment of Charles. She left all the details to
Louis, being scarcely able to talk about it, but she made the
decision—a radical one for Renaissance Europe—that she and
all her court would wear black for mourning as did the common people, rather than white, as was usual with the nobility.

According to custom, the obsequies for her late husband
were conducted without her, and she did not leave Amboise
for the forty days of mourning. Charles' body was taken to the
church of Saint-Florentin on April 18, and from there a funeral procession of suitable dignity and grandeur, convoyed
by La Tremouille, proceeded by slow stages to Paris, where
the body rested at the monastery of Notre Dame des Champs.
Then, on April 28, the body was interred in the Basilica of
Saint-Denis, the patron saint of France, where were entombed
the mortal remains of all French kings. The funeral was expensive and the coffers of France were empty, but Louis paid
for it all out of his personal funds.

Dressed in black and with a black coif over her Breton cape,
Anne sat at the cloth-covered table in her bedchamber writing
many letters. Her ladies, also in black, sat on the floor, watching. A little pet dog curled up on her train, and a linnet sang
in its cage. As she wrote, she frequently pressed her linen
handkerchief to her eyes to wipe away the tears. It was an
effort to write, but some matters could wait no longer. Messengers fanned out to all the cities, the castles, and the
churches of Brittany, carrying the orders of the Duchess regarding the business of the realm and the masses to be said for
the repose of the soul of Charles VIII of France. Brittany was
in an unusual situation: first, she had fought hard but fruit-

lessly for her independence; then she was an ally of her former enemy, but still ruled by the beloved Duchess; now she was a duchy again, and independent—but for how long? The people awaited the next move of their sovereign.

On May 15, at Anne's invitation, there was a great gathering at Amboise of nobles, bourgeois, and men of the church to celebrate a service in memory of Charles VIII. Immediately afterward, Anne and her chosen attendants set out for Paris and the Maison d'Etamps. It was a huge mansion that had been used by several queens before her, and at great expense it had been made ready to receive the Breton court. There Anne spent the next three months, writing important letters to friends, relatives, and officers to obtain advice on the many problems before her. One of her first acts was to send to Brittany to have gold and silver coins struck off bearing the likeness of her father and herself. Thus she emphasized the fact that Brittany was independent again.

During her stay in Paris, Anne was visited many times by Louis XII. He made no secret, now, of the fact that he wanted to marry her—not in order that Brittany might once more be allied to France, but for warmly personal reasons. However, there was again a stumbling block in the way of the marriage, should Anne consent to it. Louis, too, had been a French pawn. When he was only fourteen years old, he had been forced, much against his will, into a marriage with the twelve-year-old daughter of Louis XI. Jeanne, this daughter, was a hunchback, dark-complexioned as a gypsy, and very ugly. Old enough to realize his predicament, Louis had protested strongly but in vain, for his cousin wanted the Orleans branch of the family strongly bound to France. Louis XI

threatened that if young Louis did not obey, he would spend
the rest of his life in a monastery—a sentence that the King
could have and would have enforced. For twenty-two years
Louis d'Orleans, now King of France, had been thus legally
married and had perforce, until his uncle's death, been
obliged to share his residence with Jeanne de France—but
never on intimate terms. Jeanne's own father, on meeting her
unexpectedly at court, was known to have exclaimed, "I had
forgotten that she was so ugly!" The situation had not really
mattered to Louis, for he had not wanted to marry anyone
else. Now, however, he wanted his marriage annulled.

As for Anne, though she had loved Charles and mourned
him in all sincerity, his death had brought about a situation
that had to be considered gravely. Brittany, once more independent, was as vulnerable as before. The new King of
France would never be her enemy, but there were other
enemies, and her country might be invaded by foreign powers
or torn by civil war. Only a strong alliance could protect it.
Anne knew that she could not manage her ship of state alone.
She had pledged herself to marry only the King of France or
his heir if she remarried. She had always admired and been
fond of Louis. This marriage, she knew, would be the wisest
course, and it must not be delayed too long.

When Anne left Paris in the middle of August on a journey
that would ultimately take her to her capital city of Rennes,
she was accompanied by one hundred archers, chosen from
among the finest in Brittany. Her first stop was at the country
estate where Louis XII was staying. There she remained a
week, during which time she signed a document agreeing to
marry the King as soon as he could obtain from the Pope an

annulment of his forced childhood marriage. If Anne did this out of necessity, it was not reluctantly, for she would be marrying the kindest and most gracious of princes, one who had been devoted to her for years—a man so just and generous that he would be known to history as "Louis, the Father of his People."

Happy at her promise, though worried as to how he was to secure his freedom, Louis gave her a pledge of good faith by returning to Brittany the cities of Saint-Malo, Brest, and Conches. He promised that if at the end of a year the marriage had not taken place, he would also return Nantes and Fougères.

Anne sent a message ahead, calling for the convening of the Estates General upon her arrival in Rennes, and then proceeded on her way in a royal procession, though strict etiquette with regard to her state of mourning was observed. Carried before her in the procession was a platform covered in black velvet, topped at the corners with standards of white satin, to remind people of the recent sad event. And that they might not forget that she had been a queen—perhaps might again become one—she had a gold coin struck off that showed her seated on a throne, the crown on her head, the scepter and hand of justice upheld, and wearing a mantle decorated with both the fleur-de-lis of France and the ermine of Brittany. The inscription in Latin read: "Anne, by the Grace of God, Duchess of France and Brittany." Though technically Jeanne the hunchback was Queen of France, Louis had not accorded her that honor, and the people had forgotten all about her.

While Anne visited her cousin, Jeanne de Laval, now dowager Queen of Sicily and living in France, the King kept couriers busy with messages to her. He wanted to keep her aware every moment that she was surely to be his Queen. When she reached Brittany, she bore herself so regally that her Bretons thought they had never been so firmly and imperiously governed, and they loved her for it. She reorganized her household, enlarged the number of her servants, increased salaries, and retained always nearby the one hundred guards with whom she had left Paris. On the whole she behaved like a queen who had, for a time, consented to be merely a duchess, but around whom was retained the majesty of the French court.

Louis was now thirty-six years old, a handsome man at the height of his accomplishments. Jeanne was a poor little deformed creature, brushed aside by everybody. But it was in the power of this pitiable woman to aid or defeat him in his desire to dissolve their marriage so that he might marry another. Being kind-hearted, Louis disliked, as well as feared, to subject her to the interrogation that she must undergo before the tribunal that was to decide on his annulment. A cardinal, two bishops, and six prelates met at Tours on August 18, 1498, to consider four points regarding the marriage of the boy, Louis d'Orleans, and the girl, Jeanne de France, twenty-two years before. These were the statements made by Louis XII in seeking the annulment: first, there had been no dispensation allowing them to marry, which was necessary since they were cousins; second, Louis XI was his godfather, whose command he had had to obey; third, he, Louis d'Orleans, had protested bitterly against the marriage and had consented to it only under duress; fourth, the marriage had never been consummated. Jeanne de France was called to testify on these matters. As to the first, there was a dispensation, and she produced it; second, the point about the godfather was left to the court, who promptly dismissed it as of no importance; third, the reluctance of Louis to enter into the marriage agreement had been very evident to all. On the fourth point, the tribunal questioned her rather bluntly.

"You admit," said the Cardinal, "that you are deformed?"

"I know only," she answered, "that I am not pretty nor have I a beauty of body like most women."

"But you realize you are not suited to marriage?"

"I believe I am as suited as the wife of my squire, who is deformed, yet has borne many children."

In the mildest manner, without charging her husband with unkindness, she went on to state that she had been treated as his wife in their residence and that she had visited him in the chateaux where he had been imprisoned, when no one but a wife would be admitted. To that, Louis replied that he had not requested or desired her to visit him. When the judges wished her to submit to a physical examination, she refused, saying that she would have no judge in this matter but her husband. If he stated under oath that the marriage had never been consummated, she would bow to his judgment, and she begged her lord, the King, whom she wished to please, not to be angry with her—she had only defended herself as a matter of conscience. Louis took the oath, and the annulment was granted, though it would be valid only after the Pope signed it.

Poor Jeanne had been badly treated, yet there were sound reasons of state that demanded Louis' marriage with Anne— a marriage that would unite France and Brittany once more.

Many of the people spoke out against the King, but their indignation did not last long. Louis gave Jeanne the Duchy of Berri, later added other properties, and settled a generous pension upon her. Since she was gentle and devout, she used all this to found a religious order at Bourges, where she lived out her life as abbess. She forgave Louis his rejection of her and turned to a life where she could be of some use to the world. Because of her piety, humility, and good works, upon her death on February 4, 1505, she was beatified by the Church.

Louis now had the affirmative decision of the tribunal, but the signature of the Pope to the annulment was not so easy to obtain. Pope Alexander VI was of the infamous Borgia family of Italy, and before he was ordained, he had had two sons. The older he had made Duke de Candie; Caesar, the younger son, he had made an archbishop and cardinal. However, Caesar, well-known to history as a villainous man, wanted a duchy and not the red hat. He assassinated his brother and became duke in his place, but this did not satisfy him. The petition of Louis XII of France for an annulment gave Caesar the opportunity to secure further titles and wealth, for his father could deny him nothing. As a condition of his consent, the Pope required that Caesar should receive from France an annual pension of 20,000 gold *écus*, the Duchy of Valentinois, and the hand of a princess of France. These conditions were most distasteful to Louis. He felt that it was a dishonor even to consider them. And yet, since they were all that stood in the way of his marriage to Anne, he stifled his conscience and signed the agreement.

Caesar Borgia himself delivered the papal bull to Louis

XII, arriving at Chinon, where the King was staying, on December 18, 1498. His entrance into the city outdid anything that had been seen in France before—even the royal processions. Preceded by trumpeters and escorted by twenty-four lackeys clad in colorful livery, this arrogant young man was magnificently garbed, and his red satin doublet was embroidered with pearls and other jewels. He wore on his head a hat with an enormous ruby, around his neck was a jeweled collar worth thirty thousand ducats, and even his boots, laced with gold thread, were embroidered with pearls. His horse's saddle, made by a goldsmith, was encrusted with gems. He had seen to it that important people in France would support him, and at the front of his procession rode the Cardinal of Rouen and representatives of the most noble French families.

The ostentation of the wily Italian was equaled only by his perfidy. He pretended that the dispensation had not been granted, hoping to bargain for still more loot, but one of the bishops told Louis the truth. Borgia, having learned through his spies what had happened, invited the bishop to dine with him that night and had him poisoned. Aware that there was now nothing further to be gained, Borgia relinquished the paper to Louis and made preparations for a long stay in France, to take over his new possessions and look over the eligible princesses to see who pleased him most.

Louis had the dispensation at last, and with it he hurried to Nantes—where Anne was waiting. He arrived on January 7, 1499, and a marriage contract was hastily drawn up. Anne received as much as she had been accorded at Langeais by Charles, and more besides. As Duchess of an independent Brittany, she could deal with the King of France on nearly equal terms. It was decided that the marriage should take place at Nantes and that the duchy, upon Anne's death, should not go to the eldest son of Louis XII—provided that he had sons—but to the second son. In other words, it would not belong to the French throne. If Anne died before her husband and without an heir, Brittany would go to a Breton successor and not to France. Anne was to enjoy, during her lifetime, not only the dower provided by Charles, but an equal amount allotted her by Louis, who also pledged himself to abide by the charter of complete sovereignty for Brittany. It had been Anne's lifelong passion to keep Brittany independent. During the years of her marriage to Charles, she had left all political decisions to him. Now she was older, more experienced, and she was marrying a man who could deny her nothing. In this situation, she found she could be both Queen of France and Duchess over a free Brittany. How happy this would have made her father!

The marriage took place on January 8, 1499, in the Château de Nantes, Anne's beloved childhood home to which she had only now been able to return. She celebrated this happy event by giving generous gifts to various Breton churches—a chapel decorated in blue velvet to St. Nicola of Nantes; a chapel done in crimson velvet with chalices and cruets of gilt-silver to the church of St. Vincent; ornaments of gold to several churches in other cities; and to the hospitals and almshouses of Nantes, she gave tapestries for decoration and to keep out the cold.

Louis, married to the woman with whom he had fallen deeply in love, was content to stay in Brittany for all of that winter. He tried to anticipate the wishes of his wife, and, to please her, he visited all the principal cities of the province and enjoyed himself by hunting in the forests with the Breton nobles. It was not until April that the royal couple returned to the Touraine, traveling by easy stages—Anne was expecting a baby—and being entertained in all the towns with fetes and festivals. Amboise surpassed all the other cities in its reception, hoping to make her forget the sadness of her last residence there. Louis, always thoughtful, did not intrude his royal presence as a contrast to her leave-taking, as a widow, the year before. He entered the city incognito, allowing her to enter alone, seated on a dais covered with white damask under the royal standard—the ermine of Brittany and the porcupine, the personal emblem of Louis XII.

Then they continued on to Blois, the chateau that had always been home to Louis. He wished now to refurnish and redecorate it in honor of the Queen, so that it would be her favorite residence among the royal chateaux, as Amboise had been when she was married to Charles.

April marked the end of an eventful year—a year begun in sorrow and despair, but ending for Anne in the recovery of poise and power. She was once again Duchess of Brittany. She was, for the second time, Queen of France.

CHAPTER IX

The Queen and La Cordelière

WHEN ANNE HAD BEEN MARRIED to Charles VIII, she had had
the title of Queen but had not exercised the powers of that
office. Charles had wanted her, not to aid him in governing,
but merely to love him—as she did with all her heart. She was,
however, a well-educated, forceful woman, had had royal
power for three years when scarcely more than a child, and
had recently reorganized and stabilized her province of Brittany. Louis XII did not ask her to keep out of affairs of state.
He adored his *petite Brette* and wanted her to do just as she
wished. She had been in love with Charles; with Louis she
allowed herself to be loved—a very different thing—though
she admired and respected the husband who was fourteen
years older than herself. In this situation, certain traits of
character emerged that had not been apparent before. Her
almost inexhaustible energy became a desire to dominate; her
taste for luxury, a will to possess; and her simple acceptance
of her high position, a haughty and sometimes unapproach-

able manner. She was very sure of herself now. Anne had her faults, yet she did not lose the quality of charm that made her subjects love her. Imperious and elegant in public, she dressed plainly when not on display and was still their *Duchesse aux Sabots de Bois*.

In the summer that followed her marriage to Louis, they spent much time at the Château de Blois, though, according to custom, they made the rounds of other chateaux belonging to the crown or to the prominent nobles. One of Anne's favorites was the Château de Loches, enlarged by Charles and later by Louis, in which she had her own apartments. These included an oratory decorated with delicate sculptures. Because of their many journeys, Anne had traveling beds made of wood fitted with iron straps and fastenings. Other necessities for travel were a large sheepskin bag into which were put knives, salt cellars, and other utensils for the table; a second bag containing bread; and three or four flagons of wine. Inns were infrequent, so these things were taken along as a precaution. Moreover, although the Queen was sure to be received with the utmost hospitality, she did not wish to be the cause of too much trouble. Her entourage was large, often including all the children of the royal blood, for whom she took along all the necessary food, as well as drinking mugs carried in little chests of gold or silver.

Travel being a constant part of her life, Anne had a stable for her exclusive use. It consisted of sixteen palfreys, sixteen coach horses, six horses for her litter, six small horses for her pages, six mounts for her servants, and fifteen mules. Their harnesses and caparisons, made by the royal saddler, were covered with black velvet and red-and-gold silk embroidery.

Her favorite mule had a saddle in the Spanish mode with a drapery of gold and violet, a gold bit embellished with silver, and stirrups of gilded brass. The litters and carriages for her and her ladies were lined in velvet and silk and furnished with cushions.

As she awaited the birth of her child, Anne arranged her household to her liking. It was much the same as at Amboise except that now it was on a scale of greater magnificence. From three hundred persons, it had grown to nine hundred. It took much time for her servants to store away the linen— hundreds of sheets, pillow cases, towels and napkins, all embroidered with fleur-de-lis, and all needed for the enormous household and the noble guests who might visit. Then there were the objets d'art to be arranged, the books to be taken care of—her father's library and seven thousand manuscripts that Charles had brought home from Italy—and her wardrobe to be carefully packed in huge chests.

Charles had been fond of red and yellow, so the servants at Amboise had worn those colors. When Charles died, Anne had all her servants dressed in black velvet, but now, as Queen to Louis XII, she returned to red and yellow with black accents. These colors were used for the footmen to the Queen, the kitchen servants, and even the stableboys. The six pages who waited on her personally had liveries of very rich material: their large-sleeved doublets reached to mid-thigh and were fitted at the waist with yellow above and red below; their tabards were black velvet; hose of red and yellow were parted by a black line; and they wore shoes of strong leather. Their hats were black and ornamented with feathers or ribbons.

Anne was a strict disciplinarian, notwithstanding the fact

that her pages were from the nobility. Two of them were François de Bourdeleilles (who grew up to be the father of Brantôme, the sixteenth-century historian who is the source of much information about Anne of Brittany) and a lad named Estrées (the future Grand Marshal of Artillery). One day when Anne was traveling in her litter, eight-year-old François, who rode the lead mule, and Estrées, who rode the rear mule, were not keeping their mounts in step. This caused the Queen's litter to rock from side to side, so she reproved them and told them that since they were not paying attention to their work, they must be whipped. The boys laughed, not believing that she was in earnest, for she did not appear angry. But two characteristics of their Queen were that she never appeared upset in public, and she never failed to keep a promise—or a threat. At the next stop on their journey, the pages were punished as she had told them they would be, and they learned a lesson. Nevertheless, she was by nature warm-hearted, and on feast days, holidays, or any other suitable occasion, she would be lavish with presents to all her servants.

There were many, many servants, headed by Jacques de Tournon, her knight-of-honor. After him, in order of their importance, came the head steward, seven lower stewards, eight masters of the stable and many stable boys, six keepers of provisions, seven cupbearers, six carvers, four butlers, four chefs, six pantrymen, seven waiters, seven dishwashers, a baker, eight wine waiters, four doctors, an apothecary, and a carpenter.

As for the women in her household, she had sixteen ladies-in-waiting and eighteen maids-of-honor when she lived at Amboise. At Blois, the number was increased to fifty-nine ladies and forty maids. These were from noble families, and although one would not expect them to receive pay for their services, each received an allowance.

In addition to all these people living at the expense of the royal treasury, there were the courtiers, the knights, the field servants, and the guards—in particular, the one hundred gentlemen who were Anne's personal guard. These were all Bretons, sworn to her service forever. When the court was at Blois, they gathered on a certain terrace to await her pleasure or petition her favor. Seeing them there one day, Anne remarked, "There are my Bretons, waiting for me on their perch." Afterward, that particular terrace was called by the courtiers the *Perche aux Bretons.*

At this period, little furniture was used, even in the large rooms of a chateau. Chests to hold linen, clothing, and jewels, cabinets for dishes, a few tables, and two large chairs—one for the Queen and one for the King when he was present—were considered enough for any room. Cabinets in the walls held precious books and manuscripts. In the kitchens were heavy tables, benches, and tremendous fireplaces where, in an array of pots and kettles, all the meals for the hundreds of residents of the palace were cooked.

Anne's private apartments at Blois consisted of four rooms: a large hall for receptions, a bedchamber, a gallery, and the oratory. In her bedchamber, in addition to the large bed with its canopy and hangings of red velvet and cloth of gold, there were a high, carved chest on which stood two candlesticks, a low-backed chair, and a table on which she wrote her many letters. The rest of the room was left empty to accommodate the ladies-in-waiting—never less than six were present at one time—and other servants who might come at her command. In her gallery, she kept her favorite paintings, her tapestries, and her books. The oratory was her secret place—the quiet room where she could retire to think and to pray. A queen's life was lived almost always in public, but here she could occasionally be alone. The oratory was sumptuously decorated, and in addition to the prie-dieu, it contained three little tables in gold enamel, a large silver vessel for holy water, and a gold plate for the sacramental bread.

Throughout the chateau, the floors were of ornamented tiles, the walls paneled, and the ceilings richly painted. The pillars that supported the high ceilings were also carved, often with ermine tails and the fleur-de-lis. The huge fireplaces, some of them stone, some of carved walnut, were emblazoned in red and gold with the figures of the ermine of Brittany and the porcupine of Louis XII, each surmounted by a crown. Above the carved wainscotting, most of the walls were covered with tapestries representing mythical, religious, and historic figures from various countries and peoples.

In an age when bathing was difficult and scarcely ever practiced by the lower classes, Anne had the best equipment known at that time. Her bath—brought into her private room by the servants—consisted of a metal tub, beside which was a large tank of water heated by iron pans of coals placed on tripods beneath. From the tank, a kind of faucet could be turned to let hot water into the tub. Privacy was unknown to royalty. Anne's ladies waited on her, washing her and handling the towels for drying. It was a service she was used to, and she would have found it hard to manage by herself.

Anne's taste was fastidious. The chests containing her lingerie were filled with sachets of rose leaves, powder of violet musk, or other fragrances. Violet powder was most used, and it took five pounds to fill twenty-four sachets. To provide this powder was one of the duties of her apothecary. Underclothes were not worn by any but the upper classes, and one of Anne's inventories shows that she had at this time six dozen handkerchiefs, seven dozen head covers, one and a half dozen brassieres, one dozen chemises, seven Breton capes, and seven underskirts.

Except for the three years before her marriage to Charles, Anne had always had a royal income to provide her with the most elaborate and expensive costumes. Her dresses were usually of satin or velvet, their skirts lined with satin and the bodices with Holland linen. She had her own opinions about style and often had garments altered to suit her taste. Furs were important to her costume. In winter, her bodice and part of her skirt were trimmed with fur—white or black lambskin from Lombardy, sables, or ermine, her favorite.

She wore many jewels, and even when not elaborately gowned, she always wore some large jewel-encrusted pendant that would rest on her breast above the usual square-cut neck of her bodice. She loved diamonds particularly and had jewelers fashion them into stars or hearts. Her ceremonial robes were trimmed with pieces of gold plate and rubies, and her jeweled sashes bore the motto of the order of chivalry that she founded—*La Cordelière*. One of her jewels, handed down through the centuries, is so famous that it is known as "The Ruby of Anne of Brittany."

Much as she loved to wear precious stones, Anne also liked to open a jewel box and let smooth, unset stones run through

her fingers. In her apartments she kept a casket full of emer-
alds, rubies, and diamonds—as well as less valuable stones—
and when she wished to honor someone particularly or to
repay a retainer for a service, she would dip into the box and
bring forth a jewel to present to him. This was a favor no
lesser person than a queen could bestow.

The summer of 1499 passed as Louis planned his invasion
of Italy, for Louis, like his cousin Charles, had ambitions in
that direction. Though Charles had failed to gain permanent
possession of any Italian state, Louis was sure he would succeed, and particularly in Milan, for he had an hereditary
claim to Milan. He, too, intended, after conquests in Italy,
to capture Constantinople and wrest the Holy Land from the
possession of the infidels. He was primarily a warrior, and it
was customary for a king to lead in battle. Handsome and
brave, Louis, seated on his warhorse—as he is depicted in the
statue above the gate at Blois—was an inspiration to his army.
Anne was not happy to see him gather together forces to cross
the Alps. It reminded her too vividly of all her worry on
Charles' account, but she knew it was inevitable. Kings must
go forth to battle, and wives must stay at home and pray. Because she was aware of her great influence over Louis, she
was careful not to try to change his mind about the expedition
and even felt bound to encourage him in his plans. Perhaps
she would not have acted this way if she had known that he
would continue with one expedition after another, risking his
life and his armies for the next twelve years!

It was particularly hard for her to let him set out from
Grenoble late that summer, for her child would be born in
a few months and Louis would be far away. Remembering the

three children she had lost soon after birth, she decided to be very careful and so did not accompany him to the frontier as she would have liked to do. She did go part of the way—as far as Romorantin. There she stayed with his cousin, Louise of Savoy. She decided not to attempt the journey back to Blois, but she was not happy at Romorantin. Neither woman liked the other, and Anne could not keep from feeling envious, for Louise was the mother of Francis of Angoulême, the boy who was at this moment heir apparent to the throne of France. Anne consoled herself that she would soon be a mother, and though she would love a daughter, how she hoped that her child might be a son!

Louis crossed the Alps with a large army and on October 6, 1499, made a triumphal entry into Milan, Duke Ludovico Sforza having fled. Days later, while the celebration was still going on, a messenger arrived posthaste from France. On October 13, his child had been born, but not the son he and Anne had wished for. It was a daughter. Nevertheless, Louis was overjoyed. Leaving his army in the care of General La Tremouille, he made his way quickly back to Romorantin. Anne showed him the baby, not too strong, perhaps, but certainly alive. He took the tiny infant in his arms and, a bit ruefully, announced to Louise of Savoy, "Behold your daughter-in-law!"

This did not please Anne at all. She did not want her daughter to grow up to marry the son of that woman whom, perhaps unreasonably, she hated. She took the child from her husband and cradled her protectively.

After a solemn baptismal ceremony in which the infant was christened Claude, the parents started on the journey back to

Blois. They took with them as nurse a friend of Anne's, the Dame de Bouchage, who was godmother to the baby. She was approved of by Anne because she shared with her a complete distrust of all doctors. Anne could not forget that the physicians had not been able to save the children she had borne to Charles. Henceforth she would follow her own best judgment.

The King had intended to remain at Blois for a long time, but the news from Italy was not reassuring, and early in 1500 he went to Lyons to be near the frontier should his presence be needed in a sudden crisis. Anne accompanied him, and in Lyons, the city into which she had made such a magnificent entrance with Charles VIII, she was accorded a tremendous welcome. The King and Queen held court there with fetes and tournaments and all kinds of brilliant display. When, in April, Louis received news that La Tremouille had captured Ludovico Sforza, he was extremely pleased, but Anne, who had never forgiven the general for the campaign that had brought about her father's defeat and death, was only lukewarm in her praise. The festivities increased, however, and when the heroes returned from Italy, they were handsomely rewarded by Louis in a public ceremony.

Anne had been communicating all winter with the Dame de Bouchage and had been assured of her daughter's good health. Nonetheless, she remembered how good the news had been regarding Charles-Orland until the last dreadful summons, and she was eager to get back to Blois. The royal party returned to their home in April and found little Claude healthy and stronger than at birth. The next months were pleasant, marred only by a hunting accident suffered by the

King. During September, while he was recuperating, Anne took him by boat on the Loire, for a fortnight at her beloved Nantes. In return, he planned for her a ceremonial entry into Tours, where she was received with great acclaim and feasting, which went on for several days. The winter of 1500-1501 was tranquil, and in caring for Louis while he was recovering, Anne appeared to have transferred to him the great love and devotion she had felt for Charles, though she would never entirely forget her first love.

This was a time when the King and Queen could hold court in one place without worry and without interruption. Anne, thriving in the settled atmosphere, made the palace life an example of that culture and elegance for which her talents especially fitted her. Begun at Amboise, her court developed, during the fifteen years she was married to Louis, into the most brilliant in Europe.

The Queen gathered to her palace the best painters, sculptors, architects, poets, and philosophers of the day. They came from all over Europe to enjoy her generosity and the congenial atmosphere of her cultivated company. The work of embellishing first Amboise and then Blois went on under her direction. Goldsmiths and tapestry weavers were kept busy. Many books were written for her, and it was to her, and not to the King, that Antoine Vérard, a Paris editor, dedicated the printed works of which he was proudest—*The Golden Legend, The Epistle of Saint Paul,* and Aesop's *Fables.* Anne was especially fond of manuscripts written on parchment and elaborately illuminated and decorated with delicate paintings. One of the most remarkable of these was an ancient Breton chronicle entitled *The Book of the Kings, Dukes and Princes of American Brittany*. She also had executed a beautiful copy of the Old Testament, enriched with a profusion of miniatures and paintings.

But of all her manuscripts, the most precious was one made especially for her—*The Book of Hours of Anne of Brittany*. It had four hundred and eighty-four pages written on the purest white vellum, and contained forty-nine lovely miniatures, thirty frames for pages or half pages, two hundred and eighty borders, and a calendar of twelve pages ornamented with fruits and flowers and even little insects, not to mention a multitude of illuminated letters—all done by the best artists of the period. Anne used this book for her daily devotions and was particularly fond of it because it reproduced, in miniature, the elements of nature to be found in Touraine and in Brittany, and Anne was always inspired by nature. Some of the paintings were of Anne herself. One shows her at her prie-dieu and, standing behind her, Saint Anne with her hand on the Queen's shoulder; Saint Helen, holding a pennant on which appear the ermine tails—symbol of Brittany; and Saint Ursula, dressed in an ermine-trimmed cloak, holding the cross and wearing a crown. The illustration for the month of April shows a young woman, resembling Anne, seated in a flowery meadow, holding a garland. A kneeling maiden presents her with a bowl of strawberries, while another maiden picks flowers from a hedge. In the background is a castle, and on the border at the top of the page is a bull, the astrological sign of the month.

In addition to art, literature, and nature, Anne loved music. She had in her service two singers and three players of instruments, two for the lute and one for the tambourine or

guitar. Besides them, she often hired musicians from Paris
to play for her. Actors, too, came to Blois to present morality
plays and folk dances, writers to read their works, and
raconteurs to tell stories, filling the halls and gardens of the
chateau with music and gaiety. Anne loved the old songs of
both Brittany and France, as well as romantic poems and the
psalms of the Old Testament.

It was not for herself alone that Anne of Brittany created
an atmosphere of refinement and culture in the French court.
For many years past it had been the custom for queens to
number among their ladies the daughters of the nobility.
These girls were sent by their parents to learn court manners
and capture a desirable husband. Anne took her role as protector and teacher very seriously, and her fifty-nine ladies and
forty young girls made up a veritable school of etiquette
whose rules, considered by some too strict, were made and
administered by the Queen. Devout and virtuous herself, she
determined to instill the same qualities in her charges and
to protect them from too free a life, from dissipation and
passing love affairs, so that they could be presented, when the
opportunity for a good marriage occurred, as graduates of the
best finishing school in Europe. A great many of the noble
families were anxious for her to receive their daughters—so
many that she was able to select only those young ladies that
she thought would benefit from her instruction. Though
Anne's strictness suggested the convent, the court was hardly
that, and she made a point of their learning to behave properly with the young men—the courtiers—who were always
present. The girls listened to music, they danced, they learned
to converse pleasantly. They were taught to embroider, make

tapestries, and manage a household. And because of the ir-
reproachable character of the Queen, rare in that day and age,
the tone of court life was high.

It was for these young ladies, and the older women, too, that
Anne created the Order of *La Cordelière*, in memory of Saint
Francis of Assisi, to whom her father had been devoted. The
Order used as its emblem the tassel and cord symbolic of the
monastic robe. But this was a Renaissance court, and the
emblem, worn by all ladies worthy of it, was far from the simple cord worn by the monks. It was a necklace in the form of
a twisted cord, set with precious stones and with a tassel
pendant. Those admitted to the Order were obliged to promise to live a virtuous life, and though the young girls were
tempted to flirt with the young men, they strove to resist the
temptation. They were afraid of their mistress, the Queen,
who did not want them to follow their own inclinations, but
to wait until she found them suitable husbands. Few of the
girls defied her, and she was, because of her kindness, greatly
loved by her young charges. She had them attended when they
were ill, often offered them some of her dresses, assisted them
with money now and then, and, finally, provided them with
a dowry when they married. The fame of Anne's young ladies
of the *Cordelière* spread abroad, and sometimes even a foreign
prince would write to her, begging her to select a wife for him
from the members of her Order.

Anne arranged marriages with kings and princes for many
of her maids-of-honor, and whereas some went willingly, there
were those who were heartbroken to be sent off to marry in
a strange land when perhaps they had become attached to
some noble of the court of France. Anne was not greatly

moved by these affairs of the heart. Although she herself had been blessed in her two marriages, she knew that it was unusual to marry for love, and she did not think her maids should expect their personal wishes to outweigh the advantages of a carefully arranged marriage.

In one case, however, she took the girl's part against a powerful but villainous suitor. Caesar Borgia, who had brought the papal bull to Louis XII and had been promised the hand of a French princess, cast his eyes on Anne's favorite maid-of-honor, Charlotte of Aragon, daughter of the deposed Frederic, King of Naples and Sicily. His suit was denied by her father, and the decision was upheld by Anne. Charlotte was a handsome girl and had, moreover, a great deal of money. Italian servants and courtiers attended her even at the court of France where she was brought up. Caesar thought it would be a fine match for him, for he would not only get a beautiful wife, but could perhaps, through her, win for himself her father's former kingdom. Charlotte would not for one moment consider him as a husband. She said she "would not marry a priest, son of a priest, who had murdered his own brother and led a dishonorable life of crime." She was referring to the fact that both his father, as Pope, and Caesar, as Cardinal, had taken clerical vows. The Italian was obliged to give her up, but he vowed vengeance. Frederic was driven out of Italy and took refuge in France. Louis tried to make peace and suggested to Alain d'Albret that his daughter should marry the Borgia. He at first refused, but when the Pope promised a dowry of 200,000 *écus* a year and a cardinal's hat for Albret's son, he gave in, and his unhappy daughter had no choice in the matter. Charlotte was more fortunate. Her mistress, the

Queen, found her a more agreeable match with a young Breton count, Guy de Laval, who made her an excellent husband.

Anne of Brittany was not without faults: she did not welcome interference, even from her husband, especially where Brittany was concerned; though highly intelligent, she was somewhat opinionated; she was, on occasion, imperious; and she allowed jealousy to influence her better judgment when the future of her daughter was being considered. But on the whole, her personal life was exemplary. Whatever her experiences, painful or happy, she kept the even tenor of her ways, creating harmony wherever she was. She lived by the motto chosen by the early dukes of Brittany when they selected the white ermine—symbol of purity—as their emblem. It was a Latin phrase meaning, "Better death than dishonor." To this she added the words *A ma Vie,* and had them inscribed on a streamer attached to the gold collar of a little carved ermine that she kept in her apartments. The words were also embroidered on her bed coverings, and carved in the chapel at Nantes and elsewhere. She meant that her life would be lived according to the motto. At the end of the *Book of Hours* is found another motto by which Anne lived: *Non mudara*—"She will not change." These phrases influenced and guided the young woman whose power as Duchess of Brittany and twice Queen of France was almost unlimited, but who did not misuse it, whose fixed purpose was to live fully, intellectually, and spiritually, and who, by so doing, left an indelible mark on the Europe of the Renaissance.

CHAPTER X

Anne and Louis

ANNE'S QUIET BUT ELEGANT way of life, with as much of her time as possible devoted to culture, education, and good works, was constantly interrupted by events not under her control. Louis' Italian campaigns continued, and though he was not always with the armies, he was continually going back and forth to Italy and exposing himself to danger. To add to Anne's worries, the King had two severe illnesses. And it was a great sorrow to both parents that of the three children born after Claude—two of them sons—only one, another daughter, survived. A constant question, running through the years, was the betrothal of Claude, a subject on which Anne and Louis did not agree and which brought about the only serious quarrel between them.

On several occasions, the Queen was called upon to provide lavish entertainment for foreign visitors—an activity at which she excelled. One visit she particularly welcomed, because it had to do with Claude's future. When her daughter was an infant, it seemed that France needed most an alliance with Austria and the Netherlands. Philip, son of that Maximilian of Anne's youth, had taken as wife Joanna of Castile, a Spanish princess, and their son Charles was the same age as Claude. Louis' proposal that they should be betrothed was seconded heartily by Anne—she could not remember without shuddering his half-jesting remark upon the baby's birth that he would marry her to the son of Louise of Savoy—and the Austrians were invited to Blois. Philip and Joanna accepted the invitation and arrived in 1501 to sign the contract. They did not bring their two-year-old with them since their visit was strictly a matter of politics. Neither had been to France, and they were curious about the splendid French court of which all Europe had heard.

Striving to impress the French, they arrived with a magnificent company of one hundred horses carrying knights, litters for the ladies, and wagons of supplies. The procession entered Blois at night. The town was brilliantly lighted with torches at every house, as well as hundreds more at the castle. This was upon order of the King, for the people were not enthusiastic; they did not want the little princess to marry a foreigner. Anne arranged it so that when Philip and Joanna entered the chateau, they saw the grand staircase lined with archers in gilded armor, and the long hall with four hundred pages and Swiss guards holding torches. Pages led them past this glittering array to a room of state where the King was seated, surrounded by his courtiers and flanked by two bishops. "Here is a fine Prince!" exclaimed Louis in welcome, but he took care to allow Philip to make the three formal bows required by etiquette before rising and coming forward

to greet him. Then he asked, according to custom, if the
Princess Joanna wished to bestow a kiss upon his cheek. After
formally asking permission of the Bishop of Cordova, she did
so. Anne was not present, and following an exchange of
pleasantries, the King asked Joanna if she would not like to
be presented to her. She answered politely, and he sent her,
escorted by six pages in red and yellow liveries, each bearing
a golden candlestick, to a room where Anne was seated in an
armchair, surrounded by her ladies, who were sitting on cushions. Joanna, remembering that Anne had caused offense to
the house of Austria by jilting Maximilian and causing his
daughter Marguerite to be sent home, had intended to make
a very slight obeisance, but as she was escorted from the door
by the Duchess of Bourbon and started her bow, she was
accidentally pushed from behind by her escort and suddenly
found herself on her knees to the Queen of France. She was
immediately assisted to her feet, but a slight titter went
around the room. The atmosphere was thereafter strained,
but Anne, who knew the requirements of courtesy toward
one of Joanna's rank, suggested that after her long journey,
she must want to retire. Joanna accepted gratefully and was
taken to her apartments, but the unpleasantness was not yet
over. She was met at the door by a nurse holding baby Claude,
who set up a howl at the sight of the strange lady. She cried
and screamed, and all of Joanna's efforts to placate her failed.
Claude did not make a very good impression on her future
mother-in-law, but she was, after all, only a baby. The Princess
was obliged to remain at the door while a group of little girls,
all under twelve and richly dressed, sang a song in her honor.

Then, finally, she was able to retire to the apartments that had been made ready for her.

She was not disappointed in the splendor of the hospitality of the Queen. Joanna's apartments were royal; they were hung with cloth of gold, white damask, and red satin, there were green velvet stools and cushions for her ladies, and her bed had a cloth of gold coverlet. Her supper, served at seven, was a ceremony. First came six pages in the Queen's livery, each carrying a golden candlestick, followed by the Duchess of Bourbon with a gold box of sweetmeats; then came Louise of Savoy with a box of napkins. Mademoiselle de Foix was next, with a huge box of candies and preserved fruits; then a company of footmen brought in the dinner; and, finally, came a platoon of footmen, bearing a large green coffer full of mirrors, sponges, clothes brushes with red velvet handles, pin cushions of crimson satin, combs, nightcaps—everything that could be thought of for her comfort.

The royal visitors stayed nearly a week. On Thursday, Louis and Philip went falcon hunting together; on Friday, there was a stag hunt; on Saturday, a tournament; on Sunday, a marquis was married to one of Anne's handmaidens in a brilliant wedding ceremony; on Monday a great solemn Mass was celebrated with a famous French choir on one side of the church and a Burgundian choir on the other. Joanna had been rather touchy about rank ever since the incident when she was presented to the Queen. In the church at the time of the offertory, one of the Queen's ladies held out to her a bag of coins, saying that it was customary for the hostess to provide money to be offered in her name. Joanna held back, feeling that if she accepted the bag, she would be acknowledging herself to be inferior—a vassal—and she supplied her own money for her offering. Later, when the Queen left the church before her, Joanna took that as another insult and waited for a while so it would appear that she was making an independent departure. Such were the small things among royalty that determined the success or failure of a mission, friendship or hatred between rivals, or even a cause for war! That evening Joanna entered the great hall in full Spanish dress, to emphasize her right, as the daughter of the Spanish King, to be considered an equal to the French Queen. The Treaty of Trent, sealing the marriage of Claude and Charles of Luxembourg, had been signed that day by Philip, so he and his Spanish princess departed the next morning. Great expense and fanfare had accompanied this visit, but the treaty was never carried out.

It was in 1501 that Louis, having succeeded in his first Italian campaign, decided to organize an expedition against the Turks. His aim was to capture Constantinople and return the Holy Land to the possession of Christian forces. This was the dream that Charles had not lived to carry out. It was a dream that had persisted for centuries, inspiring many crusades, and it was a dream also of Anne's. She put all her Breton forces at the disposal of the King. She had a large and beautiful ship built and christened *La Cordelière*. It headed a flotilla of more than a dozen Breton ships and galleys, on which the most experienced sailors and the bravest knights were chosen to serve. With glorious hope the navy set out to meet their confederates from Venice and Bohemia and the Knights of Malta. In their first engagement with the Turkish fleet, the knights showed great courage, but it was soon evi-

dent that the French and their allies had not a large enough
force to conquer their enemies. Storms arose that scattered
their ships, and many of the men were ready to retreat to
safety. The Bretons held out the longest but, being aban-
doned by the others, they had no choice but to return. It was
with relief that Anne heard of the arrival at Brest of *La
Cordelière* and her sister ships. They were her pride and joy,
and they were safe for the time being. She was disappointed
in their failure, for this particular military effort seemed far
more important to her than the war of conquest being pursued in Italy.

As the Italian campaign continued, Louis was away much
of the time. In March, 1502, returning to Lyons, he sent for
Anne on a matter of extreme importance. Sensing something
dramatic, she joined him as quickly as possible. The occasion
was a friendly meeting with the Archduke of Austria, Maximilian, with whom Anne came at last face to face. The proxy
marriage was now so far in the past, however, that she had
little interest in him as a person, but as a rival power he was
very important, for France had been for years either at war
with Austria or competing with that country for power over
the Italian states. It was with great satisfaction, then, that she
found that the reason the Archduke had come to Lyons was
that Louis had succeeded in persuading him to make a pact
of peace. After attending mass, the two kings placed their
hands on the Bible, and Anne, standing near, was asked to
place her hand with theirs. All three swore to preserve "a
peace firm and stable and never to be revoked." It was the
first time that a Queen of France had joined her husband in
confirming a foreign treaty. Yet, however solemn the vows,

future events had a way of breaking them. After the ceremony, the Archduke departed, but a few miles away he fell
ill. He returned to Lyons, was lodged in an abbey, and was
visited every day by Louis and Anne. They became good
friends, and during his convalescence, Anne made up a game
of cards to entertain him. It was called *L'Alluette,* became
popular, and was played through many of the following centuries. By June he was well enough for them to leave him at
Lyons and return to their home. Anne was glad, for she
wanted to be in Blois for the birth of her second child.

The birth was anxiously anticipated by all—surely it would
be a son this time. Louise of Savoy, whose son was heir apparent, worried lest he be supplanted. When the baby—a son,
indeed—lived only a few hours, she rejoiced, though all
France was grieving. She wrote in her journal: "Anne, Queen
of France, on the day of St. Agnes, January 21, bore a son, but
he cannot stand in the way of my Caesar, for he had no life in
him." The infant's death brought anguish to Anne—could she
never bear a son who would live? The King, too, was sad, but
Italian affairs were not going well, and he buried his disap-
pointment in plans for conquest. Soon, he returned to Lyons
to be nearby if needed.

While at Lyons, Louis became violently ill. Messengers
raced northward with the news, and the daily reports of his
condition were very bad. Anne was frantic. She had lost one
husband after a few years of marriage. Was she to lose another? The people grieved. The cathedrals were full of kneeling figures, praying for their sovereign. When it seemed that
he could not get well, France suddenly divided into two
camps: Anne with her faithful Bretons and many French

barons found themselves opposed by the stronger party of Louise of Savoy. Louise was supported by François de Rohan, the Marshal de Gié, a French general and her court favorite. Yes, Anne had been right in thinking her an enemy. And the old enmity between the Rohans and Anne's family was revived.

François took it upon himself to warn Louise that her son, heir to the throne, might be in danger from his enemies. He ordered a guard night and day, and at the same time sent ten thousand archers to keep watch on the Loire to see that Claude was not spirited away, either by unknown enemies, or by her mother, who, having had her betrothed to Philip of Austria's son, wanted at all costs to prevent her betrothal to Francis of Angoulême.

Anne did not know what would happen if her husband died, but fearing the worst, she had all her personal possessions loaded onto three barges and sent them by river toward the safety of her chateau at Nantes. The Marshal de Gié had the barges seized and returned to Blois. He maintained that while the King was still living, these things were the property of the crown. Anne was furious. If the King lived, she would be the first to want her possessions back at Blois; if he died, they would be at Nantes—where her enemies could not get at them. She was debating what to do about an action that she could neither forget nor pardon when the daily messenger from Lyons brought good news. As suddenly as he had been stricken, Louis had recovered. In a short time, he was in better health than ever in his life and was on his way back to Blois.

Anne felt that the Marshal de Gié must be punished and she acted impulsively. She had her vassal, the Governor of Loches, present himself before the King as he entered Blois and accuse the Marshal of embezzlement and treason. Louis was astonished for he liked and trusted Gié, and he decided to give the matter careful thought. But Louise of Savoy, in the hope of putting herself in the good graces of the Queen, made a public scene at an inn in Amboise where Gié was staying, reproaching him in a loud voice for betraying the Queen, although she knew well that all he had done was for her sake.

Hearing her speak thus before a crowd, the Marshal said with a sad smile: "If I have served God, Madame, as I have served you, I shall not have a great deal to be sorry for."

Louis might not have taken action against Gié, had not Alain d'Albret shown him a written order, signed by Gié, which placed ten thousand men to guard the Loire—without an order from the Queen. As this was the very force that had seized her household goods, a trial then became necessary. Gié was convicted of treason and condemned to be decapitated, but Louis intervened. He set aside the order of the court and substituted a milder punishment. The Marshal was to be deprived of his office and his men-at-arms for five years; and he must, at all times, stay at least ten leagues from the court—wherever it might be held. By this clemency Louis showed himself, as always, a just and kind monarch. Anne, who had been dismayed by the harsh sentence imposed by the court, even offered to pay the cost of Gié's trial. The Rohans were now of no importance in the political scene. Toward La Tremouille, who had fought against her father, Anne had become more friendly, so the only person toward whom she now felt enmity was Louise of Savoy.

Happy at having recovered his health and more fond than

ever of his *petite Brette,* Louis XII wished to express his joy
and make public his love of his Queen. He therefore planned
the much delayed coronation ceremony at Saint Denis, followed by a grand *entrée* into Paris. No woman had ever before
been twice crowned Queen of France—nor was there ever to
be another. All was made ready, the journey accomplished,
and on November 18, 1504, Anne and her retinue entered the
old basilica. For the second time, the Duchess of Brittany,
again Queen of France, was honored with the ceremony of
coronation.

The entrance into Paris was planned for the evening of
November 20, but the procession actually arrived at noon at
the Gate of Saint Denis, which was decorated allegorically.
The *Heart* of Paris was upheld by figures representing *Justice,*
the *Clergy,* and the *People,* with, at their side, *Loyalty* and
Honor. Anne, of course, was first in the long procession. She
was seated on a litter and cheered along the way by a colorful
assemblage: street vendors and porters; merchants in red satin
robes; archers and crossbowmen in uniform; grocers in green
damask; drapers in violet and crimson; haberdashers in brown
satin; money changers in tan damask; and goldsmiths in
blue satin. Crowded into the square, they gathered around
the Queen while the head of the city fathers made a speech
of welcome, to which the Queen responded courteously. Then
the procession advanced, square by square, toward Notre
Dame. The streets were hung with banners and tapestries, and
the bells of all the churches were ringing gaily, yet to Anne
there seemed something lacking.

"What is wrong?" she asked Louis when he rode his charger

close to her litter. "The cheering sounds forced to me. Don't the people love me any more?"

"Of course they do, my dear. You are thinking of the first time. There can never be a first time twice, you know."

"My Bretons would not need to be urged to cheer their Duchess," said Anne, a trifle provoked.

"Remember that you are one with your Bretons," Louis reminded her. "Of course the Parisians love you. Think no more of it."

But Louis had noticed a lack of enthusiasm and had his servants find out the cause. The people of Paris held the Queen responsible for the affair of the Marshal de Gié, and for the moment her gifts and good deeds were forgotten. It was only a small jarring note in the general air of jubilation, and Anne tried not to let it bother her. That evening she and Louis were guests at a dinner where they were surrounded by the courtiers, the officers of the city of Paris, and the members of Parliament. They stayed in Paris for nearly a week, and fetes and tournaments continued daily. At the end of their visit, Louis arranged for the ashes of his father to be transferred from Saint-Sauveur at Blois to the abbey of the Celestins in Paris. This was done with great pomp and ceremony and was considered an honor to the capital city.

Suddenly the King became ill with a malady that was spreading in Paris, so Louis, Anne, and little Claude hastened to return to Blois. The illness grew worse, and at times the King did not know his wife and daughter. Death seemed imminent. The people grieved and Anne prayed, and, in her distress, she made a vow that if her husband got well, she would make a pilgrimage to one of the most important sanctuaries in Brittany—Notre Dame du Folgoat. After some time, Louis recovered, and there was general rejoicing.

This second illness made Louis realize that the succession must be made sure immediately. Setting aside the betrothal of Claude to Charles of Austria, and believing that he would never have a son, he named as his heir Francis of Angoulême, Louise's son, whom he wished his daughter Claude to marry. He appointed as regents during the heir's minority Anne and Louise, jointly, plus several advisers of state. Then he called Louise and Anne to him and, knowing their hatred of each other, he made them swear on holy relics that they would see to it that the marriage of Claude and Francis should take place. Louise was overjoyed. Anne was very reluctant, but Louis had just been snatched from death in answer to her prayers, so she made the promise. Louis then had his captains of the guard swear to serve Claude and Francis when they were betrothed and to repel with all their force, even to the death, anyone who attempted to take Claude out of the country.

Anne had yielded, but her oath weighed heavily upon her. She detested Louise of Savoy and her fat son. Claude, the one living representative of all the children she had borne, was very dear to Anne. How could she give her adored child to someone she considered an enemy and a traitor? She deplored the Salic Law that prevented Claude from inheriting the throne. She herself had been a female heir to Brittany, and had it not prospered under her reign? She was plagued by these thoughts, and her husband, aware of what was on her mind but having made an irrevocable decision, suggested that she make a journey to Brittany. She had not been there for a long time, and he hoped in this way to turn her thoughts from the oath she had taken. It was a happy suggestion. She could see her Breton people, always a pleasure to her, and at the same time, fulfill her vow to make a pilgrimage to Notre Dame de Folgoat. She set out very soon and was gone for five months.

CHAPTER XI

Danger and Duty

THE JOURNEY of the Duchess-Queen was long remembered in Brittany. With a splendid company of ladies, lords, gentlemen, servants, horses, litters, and chariots—a whole town in itself—she set out from Blois in June and arrived at Nantes on July 8. Her native city turned out in joy and from the first moment her progress was a triumphal march. It was not so much the Queen who had arrived as their good Duchess—the little "Duchess with the Wooden Shoes."

On August 19, she fulfilled her vow at Notre Dame de Folgoat, an artistic jewel of a church in the district of the Leon. There she prayed and gave thanks for the return to health of her dear husband. As a mark of her gratitude, she gave money for the endowment of a sacristan, three more children for the choir, and still further decoration of the chapel.

A little later, at one of the towns in the Leon where she stopped, a special ceremony was held in her honor. Each of the men taking part was dressed to represent one of her ancestors—from the time of Conan-Meriades to her father, Francis II. The Queen was so profoundly moved that she wept. The entire population of the town was there, looking on and applauding. One of their delegates presented her with a golden replica, set with gems, of her ship, *La Cordelière,* and another came forward with a live ermine wearing a collar set with precious stones. The little beast, white as snow, leaped into her arms and cuddled against her breast. Startled, she cried out, and Jean II, Viscount de Rohan, who was the lord of the Leon, stepped up to her and said with a significant smile: "Why do you fear, Madame? It was into your arms that he came." Knowing that it was really Brittany that he meant, she smiled and felt that she could forgive the house of Rohan much for that speech.

After she had been absent from Blois for some time, Louis sent her a message begging her to return. But she was having such a good time among her Bretons that she put him off and continued her visits. A second time he urged her to come home, and a third, and a fourth time. Finally she announced her intention to return. Louis received the message gladly, for he was beginning to fear that Anne might be anticipating his death and hence would stay permanently in Brittany. He gave her a warm welcome when she arrived and chided her gently for the delay, telling her of his fears. Of course she wanted to come home, to be with her dear husband, she assured him. How could he think otherwise!

But almost at once she received shocking news. Louis had planned the betrothal ceremony for Claude and Francis and had been waiting only until she could be present. Anne tried in every way to delay or put off entirely this unwelcome and decisive act. She called upon the love Louis professed for her to try to make him reconsider and instead to cement the alliance with Austria, as he had first planned. But he was firm. Lovingly and jokingly he talked to her in a conversation that was overheard by some courtiers:

"I prefer to marry my mouse to a rat in my own granary," said Louis.

"Truly," replied Anne, "to hear you, one would think that all mothers conspire to the worst advantage of their daughters!"

"Ah, my dear," asked Louis reasonably, "do you think it makes no difference whether your daughter rules alone in little Brittany under the sovereign authority of the kings of France, or whether, as the wife of the most powerful king in Europe, she enjoys with him the benefits of a flourishing realm? Would you prefer the pack of a donkey to the saddle of a horse?"

As Anne pursued the subject, still maintaining that her way was best, Louis rebuked her for her interference.

"In the beginning," he said significantly, "the female deer had horns as have the stags. But when they began to think themselves better than the stags, God, being angry with them, decreed that henceforth the females should have no horns."

Their quarrel continued intermittently for several months —their first serious disagreement—but finally Anne realized that she must give in, and it was her nature to do so gracefully. On May 14, 1506, Louis called together the Estates General in the great hall at Plessis-les-Tours. After the preliminaries, Thomas Bricot, the canon of Notre Dame de Paris, advanced, fell to his knees, and made a speech to his monarch. He thanked him, in the name of France, for having restored and maintained order in the departments of justice and finance in the country. He gave him the name of "Father of His People"—a name he continued to bear—and with great eloquence begged him to give the hand of his daughter Claude to Francis of Angoulême, who was a Frenchman, rather than to a foreigner.

There was not a dry eye in the assemblage as Gaston de Foix led forward six-year-old Claude, and Louise of Savoy presented her twelve-year-old son Francis. The Papal Legate celebrated the betrothal, and Louis and Anne pledged the word of the King, the Queen, and the Princess that the marriage would take place. Then followed a week of fetes and tournaments, which the Queen watched from a platform and the King from horseback. Philip of Austria, warned by his ambassador, sent a messenger to protest the betrothal, which invalidated the Treaty of Trent, but he arrived too late. And however much Anne may have regretted the alliance with the son of Louise of Savoy, she kept her peace and never mentioned the subject again.

The year 1510 saw the beginning of dissention between Louis XII of France and Pope Julius II. Julius was a fighting Pope, one who wore armor and led his troops in battle, and France was faced not only with the military strength of the Papal State, but with an army led by its spiritual father in person—one who had sworn to drive the French out of Italy. Anne's thoughts, however, were on the coming birth of yet another child, and she was hoping that it would be a boy and that he would live to thwart her enemy Louise. On October 25 the baby was born. It was, this time, a healthy baby but a girl! Nevertheless, Anne welcomed her and named her Renée. She cherished her two daughters and scolded herself for wishing that one of them had been a son!

She did not recover from this childbirth as rapidly as she had before, and she blamed the midwives, claiming that they had been careless. Actually, so many pregnancies and their accompanying grief had worn her down. She was not able to join her husband in Lyons till May, but by that time she had attained vigor of purpose if not of body. She wished fervently to prevent yet another crossing of the Alps by the French army, so she consulted with the ambassadors and pleaded with Louis, but in vain. The war went on, though the King was not with the soldiers, and while the court stayed at Lyons, it became evident that Anne was to have another child. Hoping to mitigate the Pope's enmity, she was prodigal, even beyond her usual custom, with gifts to the churches and monasteries, and she remained in Lyons under the jealous eye of Louise of Savoy, who was once more worried for fear her son would not, after all, become King of France.

At this time, Jean de Medici, a Papal Legate, was made a prisoner by the French at the Battle of Ravenna. Julius II struck back with the strongest weapon at his command: he pronounced upon Louis of France the solemn sentence of excommunication. This was a terrible blow to Anne, who was too pious to understand that a Pope could be vengeful. The clergy of France did not make the excommunication public, and Anne begged Louis to give in and free the Papal Legate. This he would not do, and he felt that the people were behind

him. Anne, still unwell, bore another son to Louis on January 21, 1512, but he was born dead. Anne was thirty-six years
old, and twice her birthday—January 26—had been a time of
sorrowing over a lost son.

However, events of the time took her mind from her personal tragedy. England had chosen this time to attack, knowing the French forces were fully occupied in Italy. The attack
came in the form of an army assault upon Calais and a naval
attack upon Anne's own domain of Brittany. The first English
fleet was victorious; it ravaged the coast, pillaging and burning, and returned home with much booty. Elated by this success, the English sent their ships a second time to the Breton
coast, but this time the Bretons were ready. Portzmoguer, an
admiral who had suffered greatly in the first encounter, was
eager to avenge himself. He hardly dared present himself before Queen Anne, who had journeyed to Morlaix to hearten
her people, for fear of blame. But he justified his former
failure so convincingly that he was given the command of
La Cordelière, which had been completely reconditioned,
and he set forth with Anne's blessing. Since the English fleet
had not yet been sighted, he gave a party for three hundred
guests on board his vessel one evening. In the middle of the
evening, ships of the English fleet slipped into the harbor and
engaged some of the lesser Breton ships. Portzmoguer had no
time to discharge his passengers, but upped anchor and sailed
forth with lords, ladies, sailors and all. The fighting was
furious and many ships were sunk. Finally the English ship
Regent, commanded by Lord Howard, grappled with *La
Cordelière* and boarded her. The confusion was terrible.
Portzmoguer gave his last order, a sailor set fire to the powder

in the hold, and the ship exploded, taking with her the *Regent*—also blown to pieces. Of the twelve hundred and fifty sailors and guests on the ill-fated *Cordelière,* only twenty were picked up alive, and they were made prisoners. Somehow, Lord Howard managed to escape.

"Loyal Breton! Let no one hold Portzmoguer's name in dishonor," ordered Anne, and her herald went about proclaiming her will. By the sacrifice of many lives, including his own and those of all his relatives who were with him on the ship, Portzmoguer had saved Brest. Anne was very sad. She would have been glad to stay in Brittany longer to cheer her people by her presence, but she was not well, and so she returned to Blois.

The autumn passed with Louis still under the ban of excommunication. Then, suddenly, on February 20, 1513, Julius died and the edict died with him. Leo X mounted the throne of Saint Peter, and, to Anne, the air seemed fresher and prospects brighter. On March 23, Venice signed a treaty of peace with France; on April 1, Spain followed suit. And on April 25, *La Cordelière* was avenged when, off the coast of Brittany, an English ship was sunk by the Bretons and its commander, that same Lord Howard, was killed. In memory of this act, which evened matters, Anne received the whistle that had belonged to Lord Howard, and the Princess Claude received his dress uniform—the green and white in which Henry VIII of England outfitted his captains.

Louis' campaigns in Italy, however, were over. Having begun in 1499 with the conquest of Milan in twenty days, they ended, after twelve years of almost constant warfare, with the complete evacuation of Italy by the French. Louis had had triumphs in Milan, Genoa, and Naples. He had joined the League of Cambrai and won the famous battle of Agnadello in person on May 4, 1509. But he had had two serious defeats in eight years. The Holy League, led by Pope Julius, had been formed against him and was eventually his undoing. Here an act of the past had risen up to defeat him, for it was his alliance with the family of Borgia, formed, albeit unwillingly, in order to get the dispensation to marry Anne, that had won him the enmity of Julius II. Julius' greatest adversaries in Italy were the Borgias. In 1513, Anne's pleadings were successful. Louis made his submission to Pope Leo X, who was a very different man from Julius II, and soon afterward the King made peace with all his enemies save Maximilian—that same Maximilian with whom he had made a solemn pact for eternal peace some years before. The Austrian had already broken it by entering the Italian wars against him.

There was still war of a desultory sort in the north with England, but Anne felt a definite relief from worry. She might even have relaxed comfortably had not the question of two marriages been on her mind. Though she did not speak of it, she hoped that some miracle would save Claude from marrying Francis of Angoulême. As for Renée, it was easier to arrange her marriage. Through a niece, Germaine de Foix, always one of Anne's favorites, she had Renée betrothed to the Prince of Castile. Louis was well pleased with this.

Then, quite suddenly, Anne became very ill. In all her life, through eight pregnancies, she had not been really sick. She had not recovered well from the birth of Renée, but she had in general enjoyed good health. Now she had some kind of severe malady of which little was then known. The doctors came, but they could do little to help her. She suffered, though she tried to hide it for a long time, and Louis suffered with her. She remembered that she had had slight attacks of similar pain on two occasions before, and each time she had recovered. This time it would be the same.

"Do not worry so," she told her distressed ladies. "On January 26, next year, you will be celebrating my thirty-eighth birthday. It is not far away. You had better start making preparations."

Nevertheless, she had a premonition that she had come to the end of her life. It had been a good life, and she had not wasted a moment of it. She remembered the thrill of discovering that the man she considered her enemy and against whom she had marshalled all the strength of Brittany until she was bankrupt, powerless, and at his mercy, proved not an enemy at all, but a young man who opened his heart to her and offered her a kingdom. She had never forgotten Charles. Only his death had prevented her from having just one love in her life. From childhood she had admired Louis; he had been a good husband to her, and she loved him in return. She had enjoyed all the good things of the Renaissance—learning, art, music, and physical comforts unknown to the Middle Ages. Her miseries had been the loss of her first husband and so many of her children, but she attributed these losses to the will of God and stoically accepted her portion of suffering. Her Breton people had loved her. There were the many young ladies whose lives she had enriched and shaped; also the Order of *La Cordelière,* which would continue after her time. Yes, it had been a good life, but she was only thirty-seven and there was still so much to do!

She continued her interest in affairs of state. When Robert de la Marck, Lord of Fleuranges, arrived at Blois to discuss a matter related to the betrothal of Renée to the Prince of Castile, Anne talked with him for a long time. Although she had to remain in bed for the interview, her mind was as clear as ever. But on January 2, 1514, her illness became critical, and for the next seven days she endured great suffering. Knowing that her time had come, she sent for an official and dictated a detailed will. Then she received the Last Sacrament, pardoned all her enemies, and as a mark of good will— though it must have been hard for her—she nominated Louise of Savoy, the future mother-in-law of Claude, to administer her estate. On January 9, in her chamber in the Château de Blois, Anne of Brittany died—Anne, *la Bonne Duchesse, la Duchesse aux Sabots de Bois*. Anne of Brittany, who had been twice Queen of France.

CHAPTER XII

Funeral of a Duchess-Queen

NEVER BEFORE had there been such sorrowing over the death of a queen. The people of France and Brittany, and even those in foreign lands who had followed Anne's career as Duchess and Queen, were united in universal mourning. Louis, torn by grief, shut himself up in his private apartments for a month and would let no one approach him except on most important matters. The King had loved Anne devotedly, and since he was fourteen years older than she, he had not dreamed that she would die first and leave him bereft and lonely. He wore black for mourning, as Anne had for Charles, and all his household did the same. And, at his insistence, everyone at court also wore mourning—even the ambassadors from other countries.

Pierre Choque, who had been for many years herald and king-at-arms to Brittany, was entrusted with the funeral arrangements. At this time, in return for his years of faithful service, his name was changed to "Brittany, Lord of the

Ermine," and by that name he is known to history. The death notice he wrote on a parchment wet with his tears read:

> This Monday, the ninth of January, the month of sorrow, full of tears and lamentations, the unfortunate year of one thousand five hundred and fourteen, at the hour of six in the morning, at the Château de Blois, the noble Queen and Duchess, our Sovereign Lady, rendered up her soul to God.

Anne had died in her favorite room in the chateau, surrounded by the things she loved. When her ladies had gently arranged her garments and her Breton coif and smoothed the coverlet of cloth of gold, all those living in the castle were allowed to pass by the bed to take farewell of a sovereign all had admired—a woman all had loved. In their grief, they berated the doctors who had not been able to save her. Then from among the procession one detached himself to perform the sad duty of making the death mask—a procedure always followed in early times. Her body was embalmed and her heart removed for burial in her beloved Brittany.

Afterward, the doors were opened to the many who had traveled from a distance upon hearing the news and who claimed the right to view the body of Anne of Brittany as it lay upon the royal bed, around which five mendicant friars knelt in prayer.

On Friday, January 13, Anne's body was taken to lie in state in a large room in the chateau. She was royally clad in a gold bodice and a purple velvet robe furred with ermine and embellished with precious stones. On her head, which was covered with a jeweled veil bordered by the usual white band of Holland linen, she wore the crown of France. Her white-gloved hands were joined as in prayer. On a golden table rested the scepter and on another table the hand of justice. The room was encircled with a band of black velvet on which were affixed the escutcheons and devices of the Queen-Duchess, among which were the motto, *A ma Vie,* and the golden emblem of the Order of *La Cordelière.*

From Saturday until Monday evening, princes, princesses, ladies, and maids-of-honor—all the household of the Queen—took turns as her guard of honor. On Monday evening, in the presence of the assembled court, the body of Anne of Brittany was deposited in a wooden coffin overlaid with lead and covered with copper plate inscribed with her epitaph. On Tuesday, January 17, in this same room, the casket was displayed on a black velvet platform, above which was hung a portrait of the Queen painted by Jean Perreal. Around it burned a dozen candles, each weighing twelve pounds. The kings-at-arms and heralds of France and Brittany mounted guard. Each day the prelates with choristers, deacons, and subdeacons of the royal chapel celebrated four grand Masses and several low Masses. Two weeks passed as the solemn ceremonies went on.

On Friday, February 3, at two o'clock, the officers of the royal household carried the coffin into the church of Saint-Sauveur. They were followed by the French princes and princesses, the Queen's household, the clergy, four hundred of the poor—whom Anne had always protected—and envoys from Brittany. Francis of Angoulême, heir to the throne, was clad in a mantle three yards long, which, as a sign of mourning, was allowed to trail in the dust. The body was placed in the heart of the church on top of a series of platforms. On Saturday, in front of the chapel, Masses were said by three bishops—of Paris, Limoges, and Bayeux. Guillaume Parvi, Anne's confessor, began the first part of the funeral oration— the last words of which would be spoken at Saint-Denis. Later that day, on a four-wheeled chariot covered with black velvet crossed with white and surrounded by four hundred torches held aloft by archers and Swiss Guards, their halberds reversed, Anne of Brittany and France commenced her last journey. The cortege passed between lines of kneeling peasants, to whom alms were distributed in the name of their benefactor. Each night the procession halted in one of the many towns or villages on the way, and the casket was placed in a church. Each morning it was taken up again and continued its way toward Paris and its final resting place in the Basilica of Saint-Denis.

On the fourteenth of February the funeral cortege approached Notre Dame de Paris. The houses of the city were draped in black, and there were lighted torches at the doors. The princes and princesses of the blood, who had made the ten-day journey on little black mules and palfreys led by footmen, were now surrounded by tradesmen, archers, and watchmen of Paris, University students, and members of the Chapter of Notre Dame. The great cathedral was draped in black and lighted by twelve thousand candles, and the casket was carried down the long aisle and placed on the catafalque by pallbearers. Present were a cardinal, two archbishops, several bishops, and numerous clergy of lesser degree. The next day, Cardinal Jean de Luxembourg conducted the service, and Guillaume Parvi continued with the second part of the funeral oration.

"Honorable and devoted friends," he began, "pray for that

most high, most powerful, most excellent, magnanimous, and *très débonnaire* princess, Anne, by the Grace of God and her still-living husband, Duchess of Brittany, who passed away at the Château de Blois on the ninth of January and is here present in the church of Notre Dame."

On February 16, at Saint-Denis, the Cardinal read the last rites, and Guillaume Parvi recited the last part of his funeral oration. At the end he pronounced these words: "I swear before all that I have heard the confession of the communicant and that she died without having committed mortal sin." The Cardinal then advanced, wearing on his shoulders a cope of cloth of gold embroidered with the emblem of the Queen and decorated with large pearls fashioned like a rose with a huge ruby in the center. The embroidery had been done by Anne herself, who had presented this cope to the Chapel of Saint-Denis. The coffin was lowered into the vault in front of the great altar and brought to rest on crossed bars of iron before a statue of Our Lady. The king-at-arms of France called three times for silence, and then cried: "King-at-arms of Brittany, do your duty!" Thereupon, Pierre Choque advanced and proclaimed: "The very Christian Duchess, our Sovereign Lady and Mistress, is dead. The Queen is dead! The Queen is dead!"

He then called for the knight-of-honor who carried the hand of justice; the Grand Master of Brittany, bearing the scepter; and the Master of the Horse, who held the crown. Each kissed the emblem he carried and delivered it to the king-at-arms, who then placed all three on the casket. Finally, the doors of the basilica were opened, and the immense crowd of people who waited outside began to file by. After this seemingly endless procession of mourners came to an end, the coffin of Anne of Brittany was finally lowered to rest among her predecessors in the tombs of Saint-Denis.

On the following day, the maitre d'hotel of the dead Queen prepared a funeral meal to which all those of the royal house of Brittany were invited. At the end of the repast, the Count de Vertus, Baron d'Avaugour, Grand Master of Brittany and half brother to Anne, arose and said:

"*Messeigneurs,* the most Christian Queen and Duchess, our Sovereign Lady and Mistress, has provided for you, whom she loved very much. You have served her loyally. Since it has pleased God to take her from us, I shall do all in my power for you with a good will. And now, that you may know that there is no longer a House of Madame Anne of Brittany, I will break the baton."

Then in view of all, he held up the baton that was the insignia of his office and, in the heavy silence that followed his words, broke it sharply in two and threw the pieces away from him. Pierre Choque, now called "Brittany," spoke slowly through his tears:

"The most Christian Lady and Duchess, our Sovereign Lady, is dead. Each of you must provide for himself." All those present wept for their lost protector and friend. According to ancient Breton custom, each one of them was now released from his oath of fidelity. Those who composed the Queen's household dispersed to go their separate ways.

All except one. For Pierre Choque there remained a last mission. It was his duty to carry from Blois to Nantes, in accordance with the wishes of his dead mistress, the precious reliquary containing the heart of the Duchess Anne. It was enclosed in a leaden box carved with the figure of an ermine. This was placed in an iron box which, in turn, was again covered with lead. The outer covering was a heart-shaped casket of heavy gold engraved with designs and inscriptions. On the casket appears a crown made of nine fleurs-de-lis alternating with nine trefoils, and it bears this inscription in roman letters of red enamel separated by green enamel points:

COEUR. DE. VERTUS. ORNE.
DIGNEMENT. COURONNE

On one side of the casket, also in enameled letters, there is a verse in Old French, which, translated, reads:

In this little vessel
Of fine gold, pure and valuable,
Reposes a most noble heart
That once belonged to a lady of this world.
Anne was her name,
Of France twice Queen,
Duchess of the Bretons,
Royal and Sovereign.

1514

On the other side, the inscription, also in Old French, reads:

This heart was so very noble
That from earth to heaven
Its virtue and liberality
Increased more and more,
But God has taken her.
Her best portion
Is this earthly part.
In great grief we dwell.

9 January

On March 13, the casket containing the heart of Anne of
Brittany was deposited temporarily on the tomb of Anne's
uncle, Arthur III, Duke of Brittany and Constable of France,
in a chapel on the outskirts of Nantes. It was covered with
a drape of velvet and gold, brightly illuminated, and marked
by two crowns. In the week that followed, the Bretons showed
their grief, as had the French in Paris and Saint-Denis. There
were many Masses and other ceremonies. Then, on March 19,
from the square of Saint-Clement to the gate of Saint Peter, the
streets of Nantes were hung with white linen and lighted by
candles bearing the ducal crest. The route was lined on each
side by rows of kneeling children. First in the procession came
a herald chanting over and over, "Pray for the soul of the
most Christian Queen and Duchess, our Sovereign Lady and
Mistress, whose heart we carry to the Carmelites. Pray God
for her soul." He was followed by four hundred merchants
and townspeople, marching two by two and holding candles
bearing Anne's coat of arms. Next came the clergy of all the
churches for miles around, from the convents, from the col-
legiate church and the cathedral, all wearing copes and carrying holy relics. Then followed the Archbishop of Dol and the
Abbots of Melleray, Buzay, and Pempont, wearing their ceremonial robes; after them a hundred porters carried torches
with the arms of Nantes and of Anne of Brittany. Then came
two of Anne's heralds, who were followed by "Brittany" in his
emblazoned tunic and mourning hood and more lords and
officials.

Finally, all alone, walked that most faithful servant, Philippe de Montauban, Chancellor of Brittany. He had served
the Duchess all her life, in bad fortune and in good, and he

was to survive her by only six months. On a black cushion under a pall of cloth of gold fringed with red silk, he carried the heart that he had felt beating against his own thirty years before, when he had carried the child Duchess away from Nantes to save her from her enemies. Behind Montauban marched the Vice-Chancellor of Brittany, the Abbot of Quimper, the stewards of Rennes and Nantes, all Anne's officers, the officials of the Chamber of Justice and of Commerce, the Constable of Nantes, gentlemen, and archers.

The procession moved slowly and solemnly toward the church of the Carmelites to conduct the very last rites in this long period of mourning. The church had been decorated with the figure of an angel bearing the arms of France with this inscription: *Rogo pro te Anna*. The nave and the choir were hung with velvet, and from the two towers of the church floated the banner of the Duchess.

The Chancellor, Montauban, entered first, walked slowly down the aisle, and deposited the reliquary containing the heart of Anne of Brittany in the place of honor. He stepped back, and the king-at-arms—"Brittany"—and the heralds ranged themselves at one end of the chapel, while the cortege filled and overflowed the church. The Archbishop of Dol celebrated the high Mass, and a Carmelite delivered the sermon. When the service was over, Montauban took the heart and, preceded by "Brittany," descended into the vault where lay entombed Francis II between his first wife, Marguerite de Bretagne, and his second wife, Marguerite de Foix. Between the two caskets of her father and her mother, he placed the casket containing Anne's heart. There was a final chant from the choir above, and Montauban and "Brittany" reentered the church, turned to face the mourners, and the king-at-arms made his last official statement:

> The very Christian Queen and Duchess,
> Our Sovereign Lady and our Mistress,
> Her body at Saint-Denis in France,
> Her heart encased here in gold.
> Nobles, churchmen, all the world
> Pray God have mercy on her soul.

Thus came to an end on Monday, March 19, the long-drawn-out ceremony of mourning for a queen who had been greatly loved—perhaps more than any other queen of France. Little wonder that the bereaved King could not stand it to be present during the more than two months of public mourning. Anne's body lying in France and her heart in Brittany symbolized her loyalty to both countries. This same symbolism had been followed with the hero, Du Guesclin, whose story she had admired in her childhood—his body was at Saint-Denis, his heart at Dinan. He was the first of the Breton Constables; she was the last of the Breton sovereigns. And although she had fought hard for Breton independence, she had lived long in France and had come to feel kinship with the land over which she was Queen. She had come to realize, before her death, that from then on France and Brittany must be one, united by the marriage of her daughter Claude and Francis d'Angoulême, who was to become Francis I, King of France.

In the abbey church of Saint-Denis stands a memorial carved by Jean Juste, the same sculptor who had made the statues of the children of Charles VIII. On a marble base, upon which are inscribed their names and dates, appear the life-sized figures of Louis XII and Anne of Brittany. They are clad in their royal robes and are kneeling before draped prie-dieus, the palms of each pressed together in prayer. The light from stained-glass windows falls softly on them, and their faces look noble and calm. Through more than four centuries these statues have knelt there, a reminder to the world that, though the monarchs who came after them were so dissolute that in time the monarchy itself gave way to democracy, there were once two good rulers whose admirers thought it fitting to have them carved as in prayer—Louis, the Father of his People, and Anne, *La Bonne Duchesse*.

Anne of Brittany was well known throughout Europe during the late fifteenth and early sixteenth centuries, and she is a romantic figure today to those who visit the chateaux of the Loire and learn a little of her history. The daughter of Francis II, Duke of Brittany, Anne was a charming and educated child, well read in both Latin and French, accomplished in music and embroidery. Her father died when she was twelve years old, and she inherited the title and lands of Brittany. However, she also inherited the desperate problems of that province — Brittany was about to be seized by France, its powerful neighbor, whose king was Charles VIII.

Anne had promised her dying father to maintain the independence of her country, and though still a child, she knew that she would have to marry a suitor who could help her in this endeavor. After refusing several, she decided on a proxy marriage with Maximilian, Archduke of Austria. She had never met him and he was a widower more than twice her age, but she thought she could depend on him for military help against the French.

Anne was wrong — little assistance came to her from Austria and she soon found most of her duchy conquered. At the very moment when she had no course